Introduction

If there is an area of growth that most pastors are asked about, it is prayer. We often get so busy that sometimes we forget to pray. Even when we make the time to pray, we are unsure what to pray. Even the disciples asked Jesus, "How should we pray?"

One of the forms of prayer typically used by Christians to help them know how to pray is the ACTS model of prayer. The A stands for Adoration. Adoration is lifting up the character and beauty of God. It involves magnifying His Name. The C stands for Confession of our sin. T stands for Thanksgiving. Lastly, the S stands for Supplication. Supplication is a lifting up of our personal requests to God. Most people add a "silent I" to the ACTS model. The I stands for Intercession. That is lifting up requests on behalf of others.

Many have found great direction through the ACTS form of prayer. Some, however, find it either too wooden or too linear. *Intentional Prayer* alters the ACTS(I) model and offers it in the form of a guided journal. Contained in this guide are four forms of the ACTS(I) model. Each one begins at a different point and is developed in response to the preceding point. This form of the ACTS(I) model tends to be less rote and more relational. It explores our own hearts and our motives. It brings us into a conversation with God.

In addition to these four forms, there is a non-linear prayer graph. If you tend to be non-linear in your thinking or simply more of a visual person, I would encourage you to use the graph to write out your answers to the questions (which will become your prayer). The hope is that the model becomes a jumping off point to continue to guide your prayer through those ACTS(I) categories. The more you develop your prayer time along these lines the more fluid and conversational you will find your prayers becoming. You will be surprised just how long you will spend in prayer without your mind wandering.

The guide is broken up into 52 weeks. Each week begins with an optional prayer study on various prayers and Psalms in the Old Testament. This is on opportunity to meditate on the content of the prayers of David, Abraham, Jacob, Jeremiah, Moses, Nehemiah, Asaph, etc. Through these imperfect men, praying imperfect prayers, we learn something, by contrast, about our perfect God. To truly appreciate perfect prayer, I would encourage readers to consider both the Lord's Prayer and the high priestly prayer of Jesus in John 17. Those are not included in the studies.

It is my prayer that this guide will aid you in your growth in Christ and keep you accountable to not only pray weekly, but to pray daily and to pray without ceasing! (1 Thessalonians 5:17)

ISBN: 9781671681224

Week One

PRAYER STUDY

Read the Prayer: *Genesis 28:21-22*

Does the person praying in this Scripture use words of adoration for the Lord? If so, what are they?

_____

_____

_____

_____

_____

Does the person praying in this Scripture confess their sin? If not, does there seem to be an immaturity in their prayer where they needed to grow or a situation in their life that would warrant confession?

_____

_____

_____

_____

_____

Does the person praying in Scripture offer thanksgiving to God? If there is ample information about their life in the Bible, are there things in their story for which they should've been thankful?

_____

_____

_____

_____

_____

What, if any, are the requests they are making to God for themselves?

_____

_____

_____

_____

What, if any, are the requests they are making on behalf of others?

_____

_____

_____

_____

Your Prayer: The Thanksgiving- Initiated Prayer

What is something for which you are thankful? (Write it in the form of a prayer)

Dear Lord, thank you…

_____

_____

_____

_____

_____

What aspect of God's character did He show through what He provided?

Lord, you are…

_____

_____

_____

_____

_____

In light of God's character and His provision, what about your actions or attitude of your own heart do you need to confess?

Lord, forgive me…

_____

_____

_____

_____

_____

What do you need to ask Him to do within you or for you or for others in light of all of the above?

Lord, I ask you to…

_____

_____

_____

_____

_____

Take a moment to pray what you have written, in the Name of Jesus. Allow Him to lead you back to Thanksgiving, Adoration, further Confession, or more Supplication/Intercession.

Non-Linear Prayer: Thanksgiving-Initiated Prayer Graph

If you are more visual or non-linear, use the chart below to write out your prayer points.

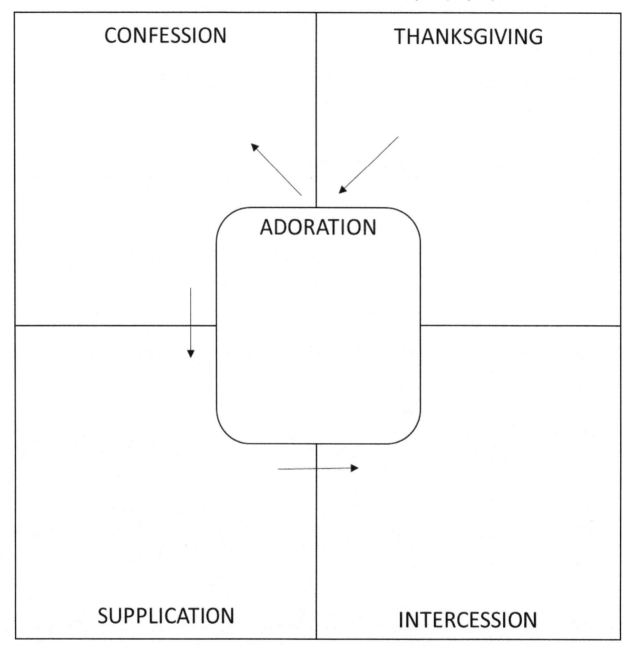

Week Two

Week Of:

PRAYER STUDY

Read the Prayer: *Exodus 32:9-14*

Does the person praying in this Scripture use words of adoration for the Lord? If so, what are they?

_____

_____

_____

_____

Does the person praying in this Scripture confess their sin? If not, does there seem to be an immaturity in their prayer where they needed to grow or a situation in their life that would warrant confession?

_____

_____

_____

_____

Does the person praying in Scripture offer thanksgiving to God? If there is ample information about their life in the Bible, are there things in their story for which they should've been thankful?

_____

_____

_____

_____

What, if any, are the requests they are making to God for themselves?

_____

_____

_____

_____

What, if any, are the requests they are making on behalf of others?

_____

_____

_____

_____

Your Prayer: The Adoration- Initiated Prayer

Think of an aspect of God's character. [Feel free to use phrases of adoration from Scripture]

Lord, you are...

_____
_____
_____
_____
_____

How do you or in what ways have you fallen short of that perfect character you mentioned in the adoration section?

I confess that...

_____
_____
_____
_____
_____

In light of this fallibility in you, where are you asking the Lord to grow you? For which brother or sister in Christ might you also pray to grow in this area of fallibility?

Lord, I ask you to...

_____
_____
_____
_____
_____

In what ways can you give thanksgiving to God in relation to all of this?

Lord, I ask you to...

_____
_____
_____
_____
_____

Take a moment to pray what you have written, in the Name of Jesus. Allow Him to lead you back to Adoration, further Confession, more Supplication/Intercession, and Thanksgiving.

Non-Linear Prayer: Adoration-Initiated Prayer Graph

If you are more visual or non-linear, use the chart below to write out your prayer points.

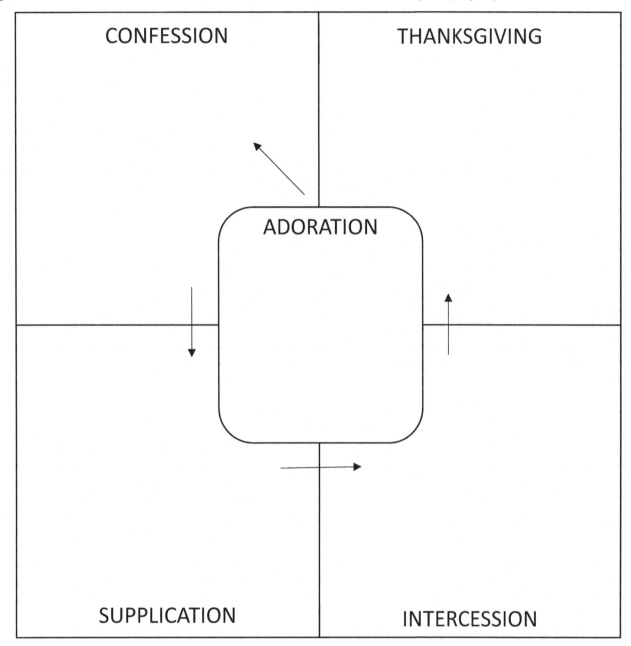

Week Three

Week Of:

PRAYER STUDY

Read the Prayer: *Genesis 32:9-12*

Does the person praying in this Scripture use words of adoration for the Lord? If so, what are they?

_____

_____

_____

_____

_____

Does the person praying in this Scripture confess their sin? If not, does there seem to be an immaturity in their prayer where they needed to grow or a situation in their life that would warrant confession?

_____

_____

_____

_____

_____

Does the person praying in Scripture offer thanksgiving to God? If there is ample information about their life in the Bible, are there things in their story for which they should've been thankful?

_____

_____

_____

_____

_____

What, if any, are the requests they are making to God for themselves?

_____

_____

_____

_____

_____

What, if any, are the requests they are making on behalf of others?

_____

_____

_____

_____

_____

Your Prayer: The Confession- Initiated Prayer

Currently, where do you sense you are falling short of the glory of God? (Romans 3:23)

Lord, I confess...

_____

_____

_____

_____

_____

What does God's perfect character look like in contrast to your falling short?

But Lord, Your Word says that You are...

_____

_____

_____

_____

_____

What thanksgiving might you offer to God in regard to His mercy toward you or His offer of redemption in Christ or His patience with you? How has He specifically exhibited those things?

I thank you that...

_____

_____

_____

_____

_____

In what ways can you ask Him to grow you in grace? In what ways can you pray for particular unbelievers to recognize their own sin and trust in Christ alone?

Lord, I ask you to...

_____

_____

_____

_____

_____

Take a moment to pray what you have written, in the Name of Jesus. Allow Him to lead you back to further Confession, Adoration, Thanksgiving, and more Supplication/Intercession.

Non-Linear Prayer: Confession-Initiated Prayer Graph

If you are more visual or non-linear, use the chart below to write out your prayer points.

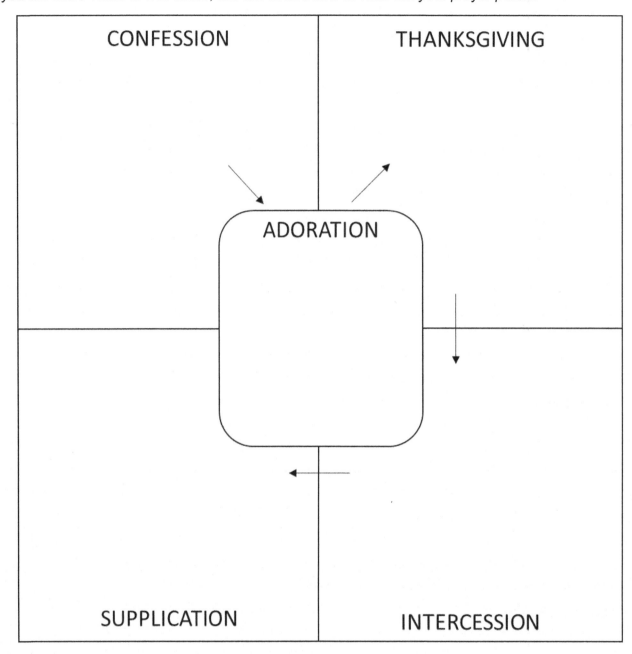

Week Four

PRAYER STUDY

Read the Prayer: *Genesis 18:16-33*

Does the person praying in this Scripture use words of adoration for the Lord? If so, what are they?

_____

_____

_____

_____

_____

Does the person praying in this Scripture confess their sin? If not, does there seem to be an immaturity in their prayer where they needed to grow or a situation in their life that would warrant confession?

_____

_____

_____

_____

_____

Does the person praying in Scripture offer thanksgiving to God? If there is ample information about their life in the Bible, are there things in their story for which they should've been thankful?

_____

_____

_____

_____

_____

What, if any, are the requests they are making to God for themselves?

_____

_____

_____

_____

_____

What, if any, are the requests they are making on behalf of others?

_____

_____

_____

_____

_____

Your Prayer: The Supplication/Intersession- Initiated Prayer

What is the most pressing need you or someone else is struggling with?

Lord, I ask...

_____
_____
_____
_____
_____

How might you thank God for ways He has answered your prayers in the past?

Thank you for...

_____
_____
_____
_____
_____

What character of God do you need to be reminded of in light of your supplication/intercession request?

You have shown us in Your Word that You are...

_____
_____
_____
_____
_____

What might you need to confess in regard to all of this? Is there an attitude of doubt that the Lord will do and be all He has said He will do and be, etc?

Forgive me...

_____
_____
_____
_____
_____

Take a moment to pray what you have written, in the Name of Jesus. Allow Him to lead you back to Supplication/Intercession, Thanksgiving, Adoration, and further Confession.

Non-Linear Prayer: Supplication/Intercession-Initiated Prayer Graph

If you are more visual or non-linear, use the chart below to write out your prayer points.

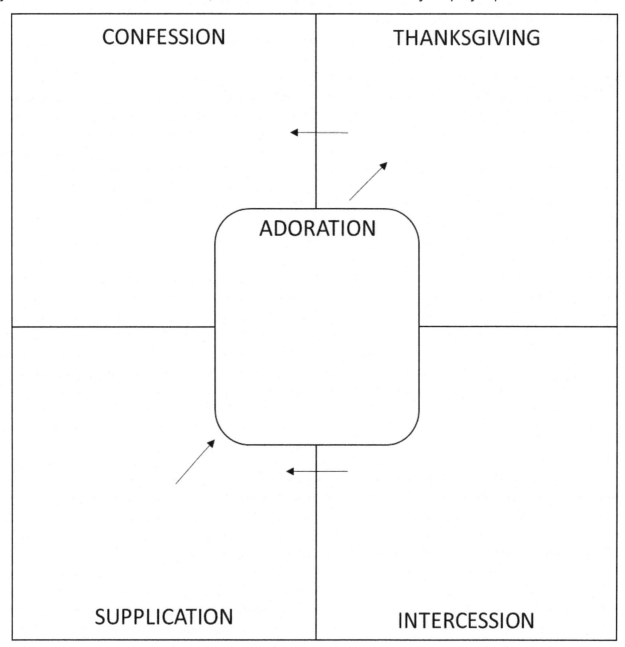

Week Five

PRAYER STUDY

Read the Prayer: *1 Chronicles 29:9-20*

Does the person praying in this Scripture use words of adoration for the Lord? If so, what are they?

_____

_____

_____

_____

_____

Does the person praying in this Scripture confess their sin? If not, does there seem to be an immaturity in their prayer where they needed to grow or a situation in their life that would warrant confession?

_____

_____

_____

_____

_____

Does the person praying in Scripture offer thanksgiving to God? If there is ample information about their life in the Bible, are there things in their story for which they should've been thankful?

_____

_____

_____

_____

_____

What, if any, are the requests they are making to God for themselves?

_____

_____

_____

_____

_____

What, if any, are the requests they are making on behalf of others?

_____

_____

_____

_____

_____

Your Prayer: The Thanksgiving- Initiated Prayer

What is something for which you are thankful? (Write it in the form of a prayer)

Dear Lord, thank you...

_____
_____
_____
_____
_____

What aspect of God's character did He show through what He provided?

Lord, you are...

_____
_____
_____
_____
_____

In light of God's character and His provision, what about your actions or attitude of your own heart do you need to confess?

Lord, forgive me...

_____
_____
_____
_____
_____

What do you need to ask Him to do within you or for you or for others in light of all of the above?

Lord, I ask you to...

_____
_____
_____
_____
_____

Take a moment to pray what you have written, in the Name of Jesus. Allow Him to lead you back to Thanksgiving, Adoration, further Confession, or more Supplication/Intercession.

Non-Linear Prayer: Thanksgiving-Initiated Prayer Graph

If you are more visual or non-linear, use the chart below to write out your prayer points.

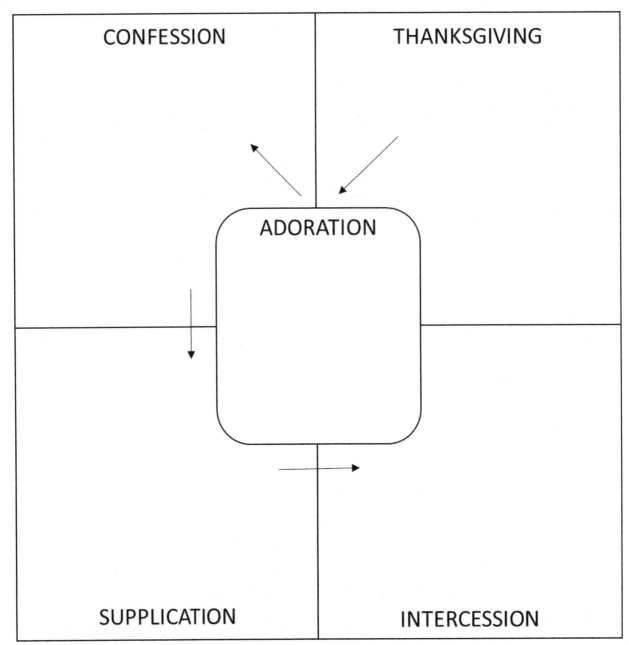

Week Six

Week Of:

PRAYER STUDY

Read the Prayer: *Psalm 139*

Does the person praying in this Scripture use words of adoration for the Lord? If so, what are they?

_____

_____

_____

_____

_____

Does the person praying in this Scripture confess their sin? If not, does there seem to be an immaturity in their prayer where they needed to grow or a situation in their life that would warrant confession?

_____

_____

_____

_____

_____

Does the person praying in Scripture offer thanksgiving to God? If there is ample information about their life in the Bible, are there things in their story for which they should've been thankful?

_____

_____

_____

_____

_____

What, if any, are the requests they are making to God for themselves?

_____

_____

_____

_____

_____

What, if any, are the requests they are making on behalf of others?

_____

_____

_____

_____

_____

Your Prayer: The Adoration- Initiated Prayer

Think of an aspect of God's character. [Feel free to use phrases of adoration from Scripture]

Lord, you are...

_____
_____
_____
_____
_____

How do you or in what ways have you fallen short of that perfect character you mentioned in the adoration section?

I confess that...

_____
_____
_____
_____
_____

In light of this fallibility in you, where are you asking the Lord to grow you? For which brother or sister in Christ might you also pray to grow in this area of fallibility?

Lord, I ask you to...

_____
_____
_____
_____
_____

In what ways can you give thanksgiving to God in relation to all of this?

Lord, I ask you to...

_____
_____
_____
_____
_____

Take a moment to pray what you have written, in the Name of Jesus. Allow Him to lead you back to Adoration, further Confession, more Supplication/Intercession, and Thanksgiving.

Non-Linear Prayer: Adoration-Initiated Prayer Graph

If you are more visual or non-linear, use the chart below to write out your prayer points.

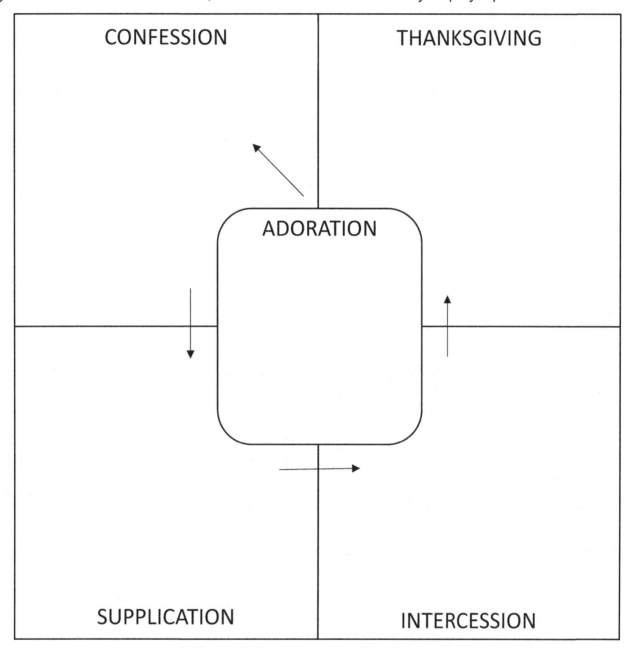

Week Seven

Week Of:

PRAYER STUDY

Read the Prayer: *Psalm 51*

Does the person praying in this Scripture use words of adoration for the Lord? If so, what are they?

_____

_____

_____

_____

_____

Does the person praying in this Scripture confess their sin? If not, does there seem to be an immaturity in their prayer where they needed to grow or a situation in their life that would warrant confession?

_____

_____

_____

_____

_____

Does the person praying in Scripture offer thanksgiving to God? If there is ample information about their life in the Bible, are there things in their story for which they should've been thankful?

_____

_____

_____

_____

_____

What, if any, are the requests they are making to God for themselves?

_____

_____

_____

_____

_____

What, if any, are the requests they are making on behalf of others?

_____

_____

_____

_____

_____

Your Prayer: The Confession- Initiated Prayer

Currently, where do you sense you are falling short of the glory of God? (Romans 3:23)

Lord, I confess...

_____
_____
_____
_____
_____

What does God's perfect character look like in contrast to your falling short?

But Lord, Your Word says that You are...

_____
_____
_____
_____
_____

What thanksgiving might you offer to God in regard to His mercy toward you or His offer of redemption in Christ or His patience with you? How has He specifically exhibited those things?

I thank you that...

_____
_____
_____
_____
_____

In what ways can you ask Him to grow you in grace? In what ways can you pray for particular unbelievers to recognize their own sin and trust in Christ alone?

Lord, I ask you to...

_____
_____
_____
_____
_____

Take a moment to pray what you have written, in the Name of Jesus. Allow Him to lead you back to further Confession, Adoration, Thanksgiving, and more Supplication/Intercession.

Non-Linear Prayer: Confession-Initiated Prayer Graph

If you are more visual or non-linear, use the chart below to write out your prayer points.

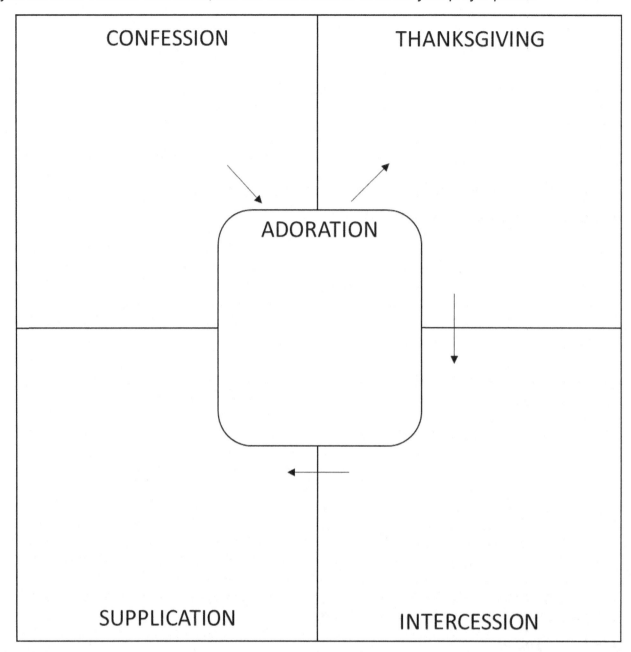

Week Eight

Week Of:

PRAYER STUDY

Read the Prayer: *Nehemiah 1:1 – 2:9*

Does the person praying in this Scripture use words of adoration for the Lord? If so, what are they?

_____

_____

_____

_____

_____

Does the person praying in this Scripture confess their sin? If not, does there seem to be an immaturity in their prayer where they needed to grow or a situation in their life that would warrant confession?

_____

_____

_____

_____

_____

Does the person praying in Scripture offer thanksgiving to God? If there is ample information about their life in the Bible, are there things in their story for which they should've been thankful?

_____

_____

_____

_____

_____

What, if any, are the requests they are making to God for themselves?

_____

_____

_____

_____

_____

What, if any, are the requests they are making on behalf of others?

_____

_____

_____

_____

_____

Your Prayer: The Supplication/Intersession- Initiated Prayer

What is the most pressing need you or someone else is struggling with?

Lord, I ask...

_____

_____

_____

_____

_____

How might you thank God for ways He has answered your prayers in the past?

Thank you for...

_____

_____

_____

_____

_____

What character of God do you need to be reminded of in light of your supplication/intercession request?

You have shown us in Your Word that You are...

_____

_____

_____

_____

_____

What might you need to confess in regard to all of this? Is there an attitude of doubt that the Lord will do and be all He has said He will do and be, etc?

Forgive me...

_____

_____

_____

_____

_____

Take a moment to pray what you have written, in the Name of Jesus. Allow Him to lead you back to Supplication/Intercession, Thanksgiving, Adoration, and further Confession.

Non-Linear Prayer: Supplication/Intercession-Initiated Prayer Graph

If you are more visual or non-linear, use the chart below to write out your prayer points.

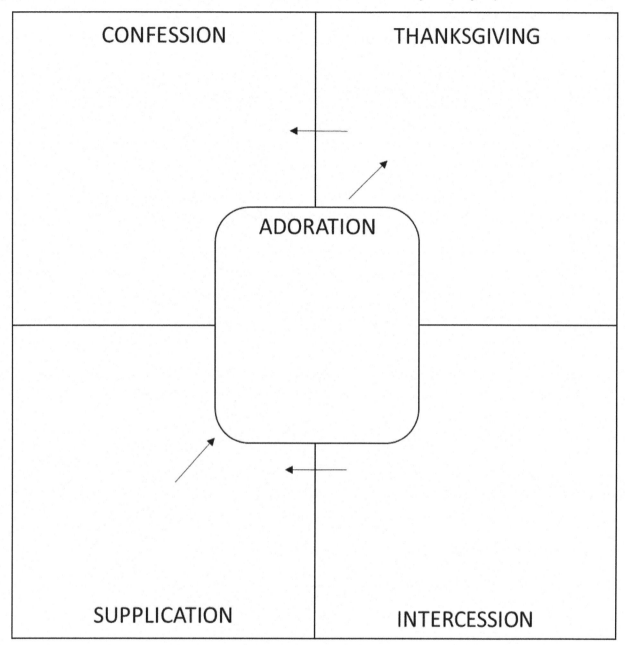

Week Nine

PRAYER STUDY

Read the Prayer: *1 Samuel 2:1-10*

Does the person praying in this Scripture use words of adoration for the Lord? If so, what are they?

_____

_____

_____

_____

_____

Does the person praying in this Scripture confess their sin? If not, does there seem to be an immaturity in their prayer where they needed to grow or a situation in their life that would warrant confession?

_____

_____

_____

_____

_____

Does the person praying in Scripture offer thanksgiving to God? If there is ample information about their life in the Bible, are there things in their story for which they should've been thankful?

_____

_____

_____

_____

_____

What, if any, are the requests they are making to God for themselves?

_____

_____

_____

_____

_____

What, if any, are the requests they are making on behalf of others?

_____

_____

_____

_____

_____

Your Prayer: The Thanksgiving- Initiated Prayer

What is something for which you are thankful? (Write it in the form of a prayer)

Dear Lord, thank you...

_____
_____
_____
_____
_____

What aspect of God's character did He show through what He provided?

Lord, you are...

_____
_____
_____
_____
_____

In light of God's character and His provision, what about your actions or attitude of your own heart do you need to confess?

Lord, forgive me...

_____
_____
_____
_____
_____

What do you need to ask Him to do within you or for you or for others in light of all of the above?

Lord, I ask you to...

_____
_____
_____
_____
_____

Take a moment to pray what you have written, in the Name of Jesus. Allow Him to lead you back to Thanksgiving, Adoration, further Confession, or more Supplication/Intercession.

Non-Linear Prayer: Thanksgiving-Initiated Prayer Graph

If you are more visual or non-linear, use the chart below to write out your prayer points.

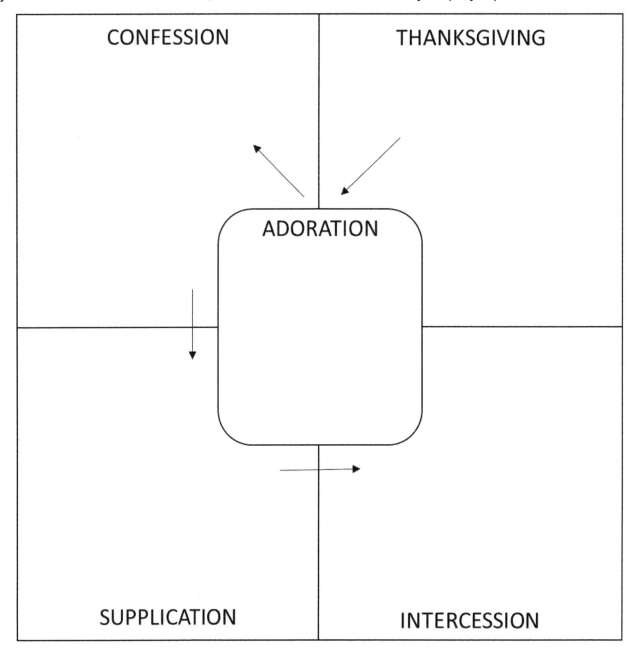

Week Ten

Week Of:

PRAYER STUDY

Read the Prayer: *2 Kings 19:14-19*

Does the person praying in this Scripture use words of adoration for the Lord? If so, what are they?

_____

_____

_____

_____

_____

Does the person praying in this Scripture confess their sin? If not, does there seem to be an immaturity in their prayer where they needed to grow or a situation in their life that would warrant confession?

_____

_____

_____

_____

_____

Does the person praying in Scripture offer thanksgiving to God? If there is ample information about their life in the Bible, are there things in their story for which they should've been thankful?

_____

_____

_____

_____

_____

What, if any, are the requests they are making to God for themselves?

_____

_____

_____

_____

_____

What, if any, are the requests they are making on behalf of others?

_____

_____

_____

_____

_____

Your Prayer: The Adoration- Initiated Prayer

Think of an aspect of God's character. [Feel free to use phrases of adoration from Scripture]

Lord, you are…

_____
_____
_____
_____
_____

How do you or in what ways have you fallen short of that perfect character you mentioned in the adoration section?

I confess that…

_____
_____
_____
_____
_____

In light of this fallibility in you, where are you asking the Lord to grow you? For which brother or sister in Christ might you also pray to grow in this area of fallibility?

Lord, I ask you to…

_____
_____
_____
_____
_____

In what ways can you give thanksgiving to God in relation to all of this?

Lord, I ask you to…

_____
_____
_____
_____
_____

Take a moment to pray what you have written, in the Name of Jesus. Allow Him to lead you back to Adoration, further Confession, more Supplication/Intercession, and Thanksgiving.

Non-Linear Prayer: Adoration-Initiated Prayer Graph

If you are more visual or non-linear, use the chart below to write out your prayer points.

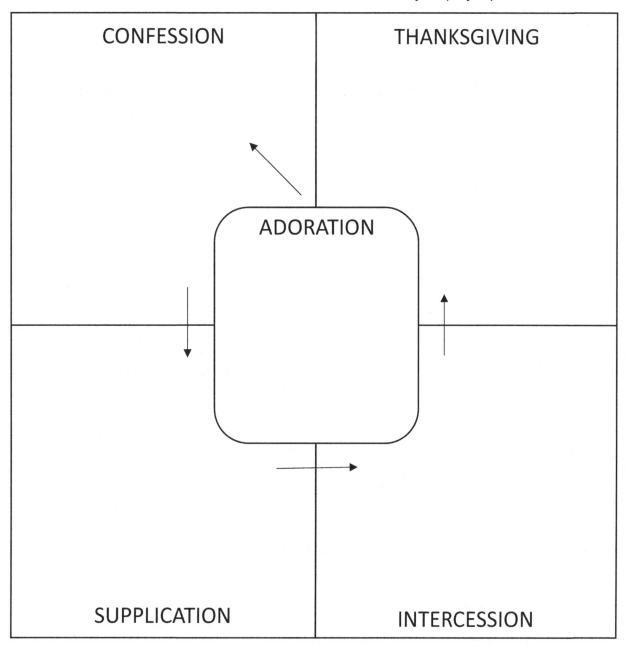

Week Eleven

Week Of:

PRAYER STUDY

Read the Prayer: *1 Kings 8:22-52*

Does the person praying in this Scripture use words of adoration for the Lord? If so, what are they?

_____

_____

_____

_____

_____

Does the person praying in this Scripture confess their sin? If not, does there seem to be an immaturity in their prayer where they needed to grow or a situation in their life that would warrant confession?

_____

_____

_____

_____

_____

Does the person praying in Scripture offer thanksgiving to God? If there is ample information about their life in the Bible, are there things in their story for which they should've been thankful?

_____

_____

_____

_____

_____

What, if any, are the requests they are making to God for themselves?

_____

_____

_____

_____

_____

What, if any, are the requests they are making on behalf of others?

_____

_____

_____

_____

_____

Your Prayer: The Confession- Initiated Prayer

Currently, where do you sense you are falling short of the glory of God? (Romans 3:23)

Lord, I confess…

_____

_____

_____

_____

_____

What does God's perfect character look like in contrast to your falling short?

But Lord, Your Word says that You are…

_____

_____

_____

_____

_____

What thanksgiving might you offer to God in regard to His mercy toward you or His offer of redemption in Christ or His patience with you? How has He specifically exhibited those things?

I thank you that…

_____

_____

_____

_____

_____

In what ways can you ask Him to grow you in grace? In what ways can you pray for particular unbelievers to recognize their own sin and trust in Christ alone?

Lord, I ask you to…

_____

_____

_____

_____

_____

Take a moment to pray what you have written, in the Name of Jesus. Allow Him to lead you back to further Confession, Adoration, Thanksgiving, and more Supplication/Intercession.

Non-Linear Prayer: Confession-Initiated Prayer Graph

If you are more visual or non-linear, use the chart below to write out your prayer points.

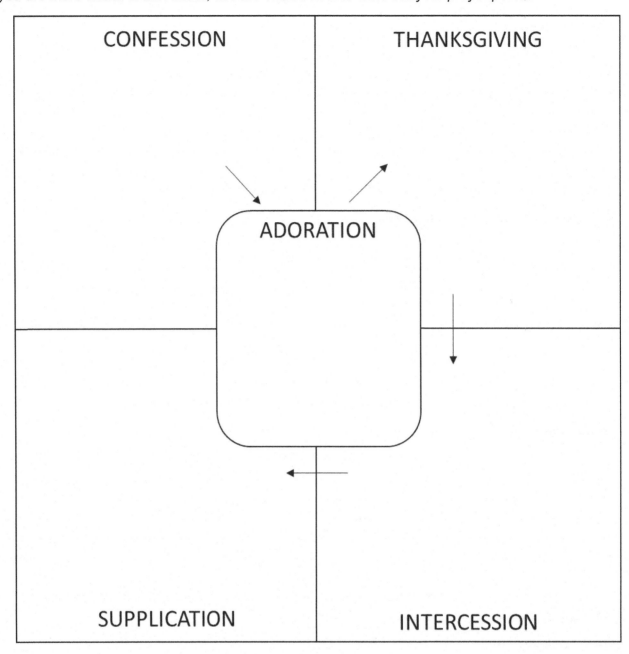

Week Twelve

Week Of:

PRAYER STUDY

Read the Prayer: *2 Samuel 7:18-29*

Does the person praying in this Scripture use words of adoration for the Lord? If so, what are they?

_____

_____

_____

_____

_____

Does the person praying in this Scripture confess their sin? If not, does there seem to be an immaturity in their prayer where they needed to grow or a situation in their life that would warrant confession?

_____

_____

_____

_____

_____

Does the person praying in Scripture offer thanksgiving to God? If there is ample information about their life in the Bible, are there things in their story for which they should've been thankful?

_____

_____

_____

_____

_____

What, if any, are the requests they are making to God for themselves?

_____

_____

_____

_____

_____

What, if any, are the requests they are making on behalf of others?

_____

_____

_____

_____

Your Prayer: The Supplication/Intersession- Initiated Prayer

What is the most pressing need you or someone else is struggling with?

Lord, I ask...

_____
_____
_____
_____
_____

How might you thank God for ways He has answered your prayers in the past?

Thank you for...

_____
_____
_____
_____
_____

What character of God do you need to be reminded of in light of your supplication/intercession request?

You have shown us in Your Word that You are...

_____
_____
_____
_____
_____

What might you need to confess in regard to all of this? Is there an attitude of doubt that the Lord will do and be all He has said He will do and be, etc?

Forgive me...

_____
_____
_____
_____
_____

Take a moment to pray what you have written, in the Name of Jesus. Allow Him to lead you back to Supplication/Intercession, Thanksgiving, Adoration, and further Confession.

Non-Linear Prayer: Supplication/Intercession-Initiated Prayer Graph

If you are more visual or non-linear, use the chart below to write out your prayer points.

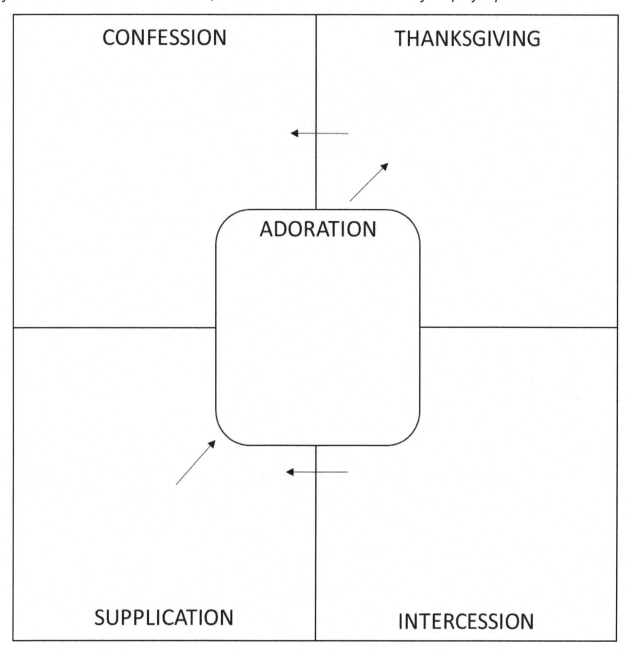

Week Thirteen

PRAYER STUDY

Read the Prayer: *Psalm 75*

Does the person praying in this Scripture use words of adoration for the Lord? If so, what are they?

_____

_____

_____

_____

_____

Does the person praying in this Scripture confess their sin? If not, does there seem to be an immaturity in their prayer where they needed to grow or a situation in their life that would warrant confession?

_____

_____

_____

_____

_____

Does the person praying in Scripture offer thanksgiving to God? If there is ample information about their life in the Bible, are there things in their story for which they should've been thankful?

_____

_____

_____

_____

_____

What, if any, are the requests they are making to God for themselves?

_____

_____

_____

_____

_____

What, if any, are the requests they are making on behalf of others?

_____

_____

_____

_____

_____

Your Prayer: The Thanksgiving- Initiated Prayer

What is something for which you are thankful? (Write it in the form of a prayer)

Dear Lord, thank you...

_____
_____
_____
_____
_____

What aspect of God's character did He show through what He provided?

Lord, you are...

_____
_____
_____
_____
_____

In light of God's character and His provision, what about your actions or attitude of your own heart do you need to confess?

Lord, forgive me...

_____
_____
_____
_____
_____

What do you need to ask Him to do within you or for you or for others in light of all of the above?

Lord, I ask you to...

_____
_____
_____
_____
_____

Take a moment to pray what you have written, in the Name of Jesus. Allow Him to lead you back to Thanksgiving, Adoration, further Confession, or more Supplication/Intercession.

Non-Linear Prayer: Thanksgiving-Initiated Prayer Graph

If you are more visual or non-linear, use the chart below to write out your prayer points.

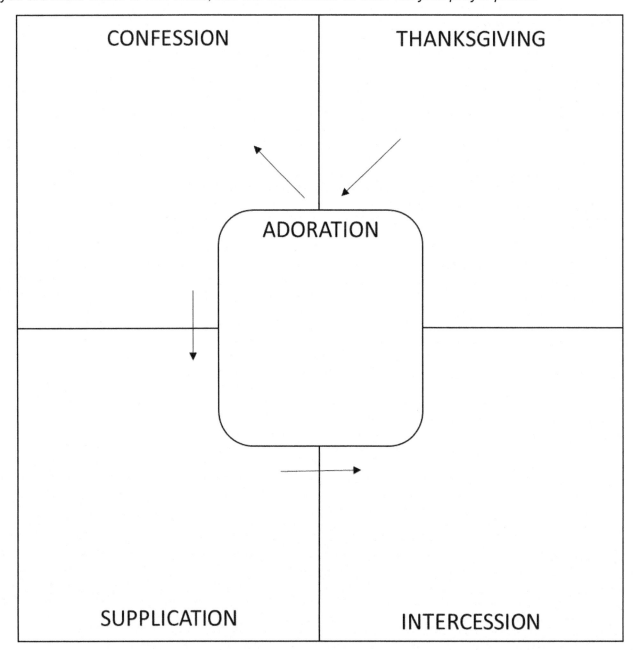

Week Fourteen

PRAYER STUDY

Read the Prayer: *Psalm 30*

Does the person praying in this Scripture use words of adoration for the Lord? If so, what are they?

_____

_____

_____

_____

Does the person praying in this Scripture confess their sin? If not, does there seem to be an immaturity in their prayer where they needed to grow or a situation in their life that would warrant confession?

_____

_____

_____

_____

Does the person praying in Scripture offer thanksgiving to God? If there is ample information about their life in the Bible, are there things in their story for which they should've been thankful?

_____

_____

_____

_____

What, if any, are the requests they are making to God for themselves?

_____

_____

_____

_____

What, if any, are the requests they are making on behalf of others?

_____

_____

_____

_____

Your Prayer: The Adoration- Initiated Prayer

Think of an aspect of God's character. [Feel free to use phrases of adoration from Scripture]

Lord, you are...

_____

_____

_____

_____

_____

How do you or in what ways have you fallen short of that perfect character you mentioned in the adoration section?

I confess that...

_____

_____

_____

_____

_____

In light of this fallibility in you, where are you asking the Lord to grow you? For which brother or sister in Christ might you also pray to grow in this area of fallibility?

Lord, I ask you to...

_____

_____

_____

_____

_____

In what ways can you give thanksgiving to God in relation to all of this?

Lord, I ask you to...

_____

_____

_____

_____

_____

Take a moment to pray what you have written, in the Name of Jesus. Allow Him to lead you back to Adoration, further Confession, more Supplication/Intercession, and Thanksgiving.

Non-Linear Prayer: Adoration-Initiated Prayer Graph

If you are more visual or non-linear, use the chart below to write out your prayer points.

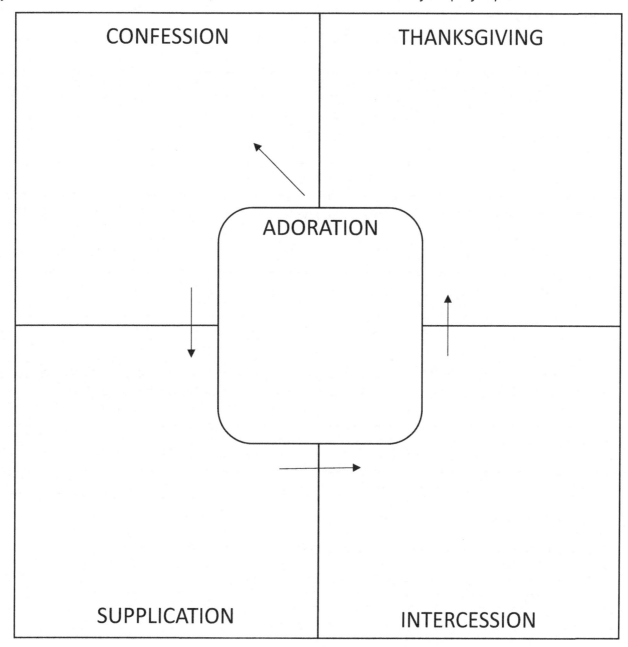

Week Fifteen

PRAYER STUDY

Read the Prayer: *Psalm 28*

Does the person praying in this Scripture use words of adoration for the Lord? If so, what are they?

_____

_____

_____

_____

_____

Does the person praying in this Scripture confess their sin? If not, does there seem to be an immaturity in their prayer where they needed to grow or a situation in their life that would warrant confession?

_____

_____

_____

_____

_____

Does the person praying in Scripture offer thanksgiving to God? If there is ample information about their life in the Bible, are there things in their story for which they should've been thankful?

_____

_____

_____

_____

_____

What, if any, are the requests they are making to God for themselves?

_____

_____

_____

_____

_____

What, if any, are the requests they are making on behalf of others?

_____

_____

_____

_____

_____

Your Prayer: The Confession- Initiated Prayer

Currently, where do you sense you are falling short of the glory of God? (Romans 3:23)

Lord, I confess...

_____

_____

_____

_____

_____

What does God's perfect character look like in contrast to your falling short?

But Lord, Your Word says that You are...

_____

_____

_____

_____

_____

What thanksgiving might you offer to God in regard to His mercy toward you or His offer of redemption in Christ or His patience with you? How has He specifically exhibited those things?

I thank you that...

_____

_____

_____

_____

_____

In what ways can you ask Him to grow you in grace? In what ways can you pray for particular unbelievers to recognize their own sin and trust in Christ alone?

Lord, I ask you to...

_____

_____

_____

_____

_____

Take a moment to pray what you have written, in the Name of Jesus. Allow Him to lead you back to further Confession, Adoration, Thanksgiving, and more Supplication/Intercession.

Non-Linear Prayer: Confession-Initiated Prayer Graph

If you are more visual or non-linear, use the chart below to write out your prayer points.

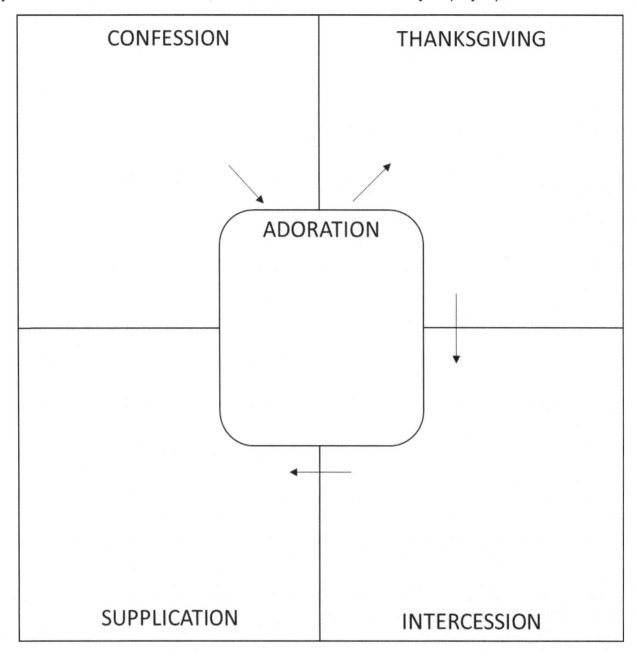

Week Sixteen

Week Of:

PRAYER STUDY

Read the Prayer: *Psalm 13*

Does the person praying in this Scripture use words of adoration for the Lord? If so, what are they?

_____

_____

_____

_____

_____

Does the person praying in this Scripture confess their sin? If not, does there seem to be an immaturity in their prayer where they needed to grow or a situation in their life that would warrant confession?

_____

_____

_____

_____

_____

Does the person praying in Scripture offer thanksgiving to God? If there is ample information about their life in the Bible, are there things in their story for which they should've been thankful?

_____

_____

_____

_____

_____

What, if any, are the requests they are making to God for themselves?

_____

_____

_____

_____

_____

What, if any, are the requests they are making on behalf of others?

_____

_____

_____

_____

_____

Your Prayer: The Supplication/Intersession- Initiated Prayer

What is the most pressing need you or someone else is struggling with?

Lord, I ask...

_____

_____

_____

_____

_____

How might you thank God for ways He has answered your prayers in the past?

Thank you for...

_____

_____

_____

_____

_____

What character of God do you need to be reminded of in light of your supplication/intercession request?

You have shown us in Your Word that You are...

_____

_____

_____

_____

_____

What might you need to confess in regard to all of this? Is there an attitude of doubt that the Lord will do and be all He has said He will do and be, etc?

Forgive me...

_____

_____

_____

_____

_____

Take a moment to pray what you have written, in the Name of Jesus. Allow Him to lead you back to Supplication/Intercession, Thanksgiving, Adoration, and further Confession.

Non-Linear Prayer: Supplication/Intercession-Initiated Prayer Graph

If you are more visual or non-linear, use the chart below to write out your prayer points.

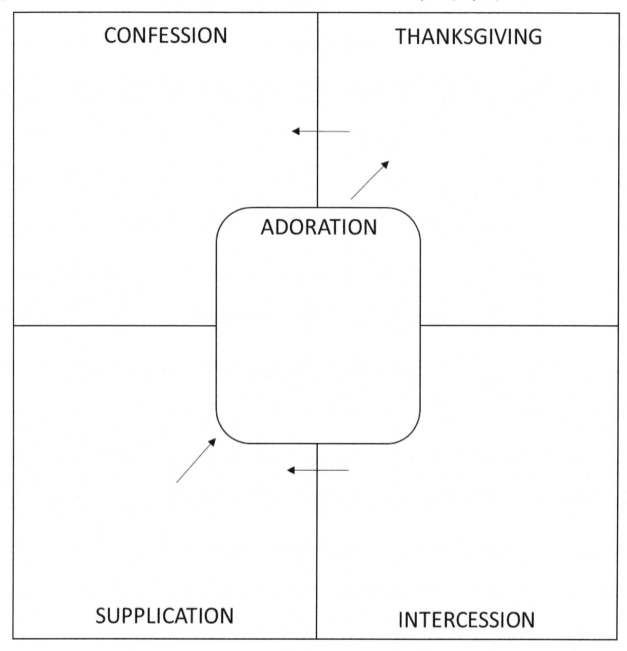

Week Seventeen

PRAYER STUDY

Read the Prayer: *Psalm 80*

Does the person praying in this Scripture use words of adoration for the Lord? If so, what are they?

_____

_____

_____

_____

_____

Does the person praying in this Scripture confess their sin? If not, does there seem to be an immaturity in their prayer where they needed to grow or a situation in their life that would warrant confession?

_____

_____

_____

_____

_____

Does the person praying in Scripture offer thanksgiving to God? If there is ample information about their life in the Bible, are there things in their story for which they should've been thankful?

_____

_____

_____

_____

_____

What, if any, are the requests they are making to God for themselves?

_____

_____

_____

_____

_____

What, if any, are the requests they are making on behalf of others?

_____

_____

_____

_____

_____

Your Prayer: The Thanksgiving- Initiated Prayer

What is something for which you are thankful? (Write it in the form of a prayer)

Dear Lord, thank you…

_____

_____

_____

_____

_____

What aspect of God's character did He show through what He provided?

Lord, you are…

_____

_____

_____

_____

_____

In light of God's character and His provision, what about your actions or attitude of your own heart do you need to confess?

Lord, forgive me…

_____

_____

_____

_____

_____

What do you need to ask Him to do within you or for you or for others in light of all of the above?

Lord, I ask you to…

_____

_____

_____

_____

_____

Take a moment to pray what you have written, in the Name of Jesus. Allow Him to lead you back to Thanksgiving, Adoration, further Confession, or more Supplication/Intercession.

Non-Linear Prayer: Thanksgiving-Initiated Prayer Graph

If you are more visual or non-linear, use the chart below to write out your prayer points.

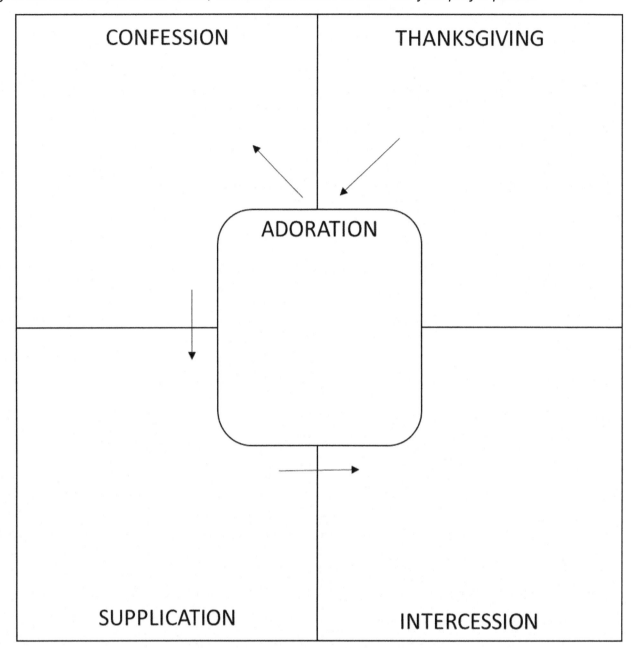

Week Eighteen

PRAYER STUDY

Read the Prayer: *Psalm 109*

Does the person praying in this Scripture use words of adoration for the Lord? If so, what are they?

_____

_____

_____

_____

_____

Does the person praying in this Scripture confess their sin? If not, does there seem to be an immaturity in their prayer where they needed to grow or a situation in their life that would warrant confession?

_____

_____

_____

_____

_____

Does the person praying in Scripture offer thanksgiving to God? If there is ample information about their life in the Bible, are there things in their story for which they should've been thankful?

_____

_____

_____

_____

_____

What, if any, are the requests they are making to God for themselves?

_____

_____

_____

_____

_____

What, if any, are the requests they are making on behalf of others?

_____

_____

_____

_____

_____

Your Prayer: The Adoration- Initiated Prayer

Think of an aspect of God's character. [Feel free to use phrases of adoration from Scripture]

Lord, you are...

_____
_____
_____
_____
_____

How do you or in what ways have you fallen short of that perfect character you mentioned in the adoration section?

I confess that...

_____
_____
_____
_____
_____

In light of this fallibility in you, where are you asking the Lord to grow you? For which brother or sister in Christ might you also pray to grow in this area of fallibility?

Lord, I ask you to...

_____
_____
_____
_____
_____

In what ways can you give thanksgiving to God in relation to all of this?

Lord, I ask you to...

_____
_____
_____
_____
_____

Take a moment to pray what you have written, in the Name of Jesus. Allow Him to lead you back to Adoration, further Confession, more Supplication/Intercession, and Thanksgiving.

Non-Linear Prayer: Adoration-Initiated Prayer Graph

If you are more visual or non-linear, use the chart below to write out your prayer points.

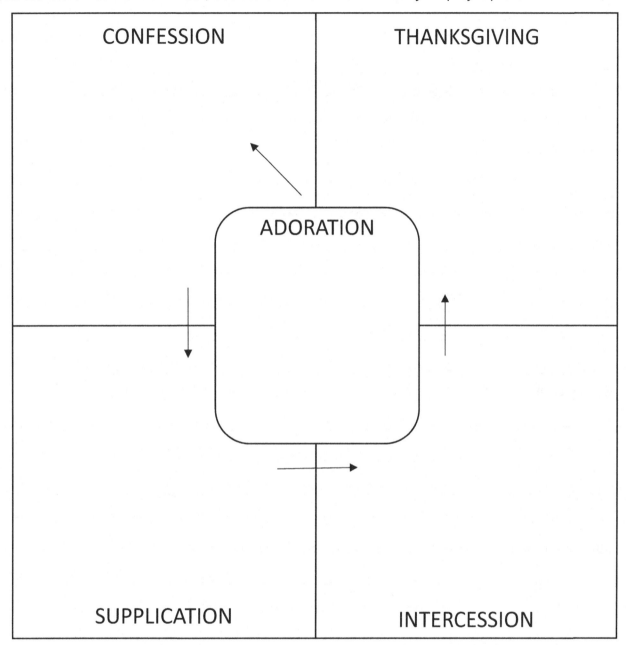

Week Nineteen

PRAYER STUDY

Read the Prayer: *Psalm 115*

Does the person praying in this Scripture use words of adoration for the Lord? If so, what are they?

_____

_____

_____

_____

_____

Does the person praying in this Scripture confess their sin? If not, does there seem to be an immaturity in their prayer where they needed to grow or a situation in their life that would warrant confession?

_____

_____

_____

_____

_____

Does the person praying in Scripture offer thanksgiving to God? If there is ample information about their life in the Bible, are there things in their story for which they should've been thankful?

_____

_____

_____

_____

_____

What, if any, are the requests they are making to God for themselves?

_____

_____

_____

_____

_____

What, if any, are the requests they are making on behalf of others?

_____

_____

_____

_____

_____

Your Prayer: The Confession- Initiated Prayer

Currently, where do you sense you are falling short of the glory of God? (Romans 3:23)

Lord, I confess...

_____

_____

_____

_____

_____

What does God's perfect character look like in contrast to your falling short?

But Lord, Your Word says that You are...

_____

_____

_____

_____

_____

What thanksgiving might you offer to God in regard to His mercy toward you or His offer of redemption in Christ or His patience with you? How has He specifically exhibited those things?

I thank you that...

_____

_____

_____

_____

_____

In what ways can you ask Him to grow you in grace? In what ways can you pray for particular unbelievers to recognize their own sin and trust in Christ alone?

Lord, I ask you to...

_____

_____

_____

_____

_____

Take a moment to pray what you have written, in the Name of Jesus. Allow Him to lead you back to further Confession, Adoration, Thanksgiving, and more Supplication/Intercession.

Non-Linear Prayer: Confession-Initiated Prayer Graph

If you are more visual or non-linear, use the chart below to write out your prayer points.

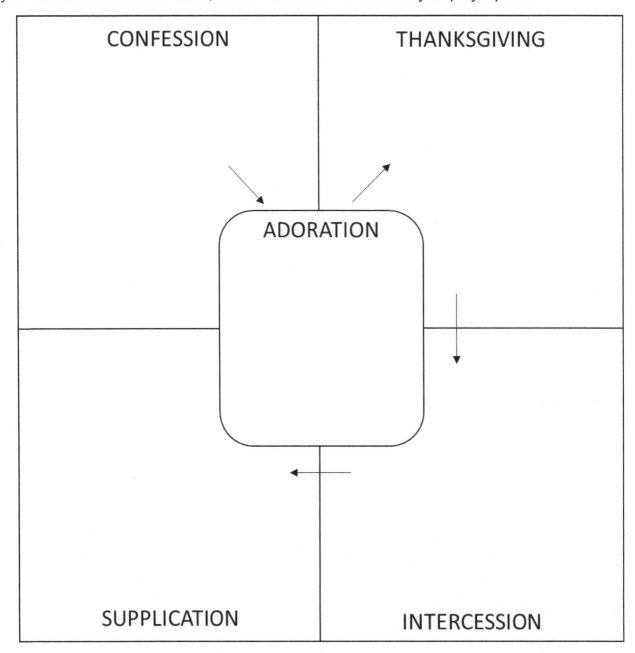

Week Twenty

Week Of:

PRAYER STUDY

Read the Prayer: *Psalm 130*

Does the person praying in this Scripture use words of adoration for the Lord? If so, what are they?

_____

_____

_____

_____

_____

Does the person praying in this Scripture confess their sin? If not, does there seem to be an immaturity in their prayer where they needed to grow or a situation in their life that would warrant confession?

_____

_____

_____

_____

_____

Does the person praying in Scripture offer thanksgiving to God? If there is ample information about their life in the Bible, are there things in their story for which they should've been thankful?

_____

_____

_____

_____

_____

What, if any, are the requests they are making to God for themselves?

_____

_____

_____

_____

_____

What, if any, are the requests they are making on behalf of others?

_____

_____

_____

_____

_____

Your Prayer: The Supplication/Intersession- Initiated Prayer

What is the most pressing need you or someone else is struggling with?

Lord, I ask...

_____

_____

_____

_____

_____

How might you thank God for ways He has answered your prayers in the past?

Thank you for...

_____

_____

_____

_____

_____

What character of God do you need to be reminded of in light of your supplication/intercession request?

You have shown us in Your Word that You are...

_____

_____

_____

_____

_____

What might you need to confess in regard to all of this? Is there an attitude of doubt that the Lord will do and be all He has said He will do and be, etc?

Forgive me...

_____

_____

_____

_____

_____

Take a moment to pray what you have written, in the Name of Jesus. Allow Him to lead you back to Supplication/Intercession, Thanksgiving, Adoration, and further Confession.

Non-Linear Prayer: Supplication/Intercession-Initiated Prayer Graph

If you are more visual or non-linear, use the chart below to write out your prayer points.

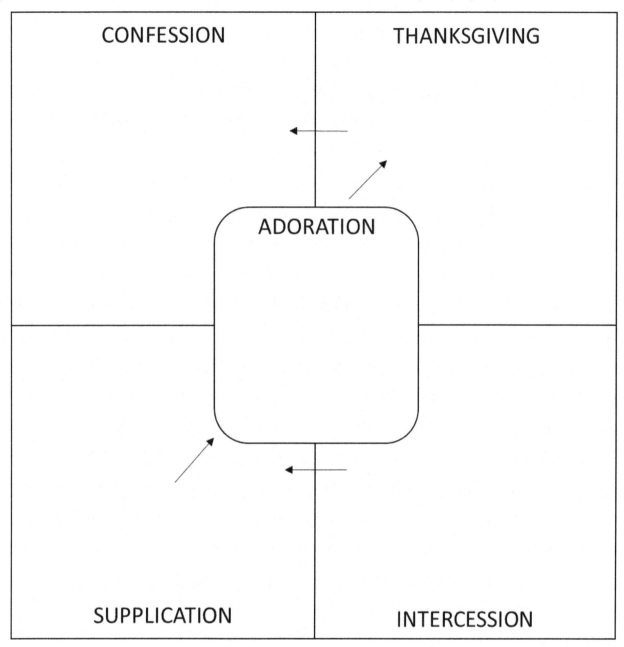

Week Twenty-One

Week Of:

PRAYER STUDY

Read the Prayer: *Psalm 43*

Does the person praying in this Scripture use words of adoration for the Lord? If so, what are they?

_____

_____

_____

_____

_____

Does the person praying in this Scripture confess their sin? If not, does there seem to be an immaturity in their prayer where they needed to grow or a situation in their life that would warrant confession?

_____

_____

_____

_____

_____

Does the person praying in Scripture offer thanksgiving to God? If there is ample information about their life in the Bible, are there things in their story for which they should've been thankful?

_____

_____

_____

_____

_____

What, if any, are the requests they are making to God for themselves?

_____

_____

_____

_____

_____

What, if any, are the requests they are making on behalf of others?

_____

_____

_____

_____

_____

Your Prayer: The Thanksgiving- Initiated Prayer

What is something for which you are thankful? (Write it in the form of a prayer)

Dear Lord, thank you...

_____

_____

_____

_____

_____

What aspect of God's character did He show through what He provided?

Lord, you are...

_____

_____

_____

_____

_____

In light of God's character and His provision, what about your actions or attitude of your own heart do you need to confess?

Lord, forgive me...

_____

_____

_____

_____

_____

What do you need to ask Him to do within you or for you or for others in light of all of the above?

Lord, I ask you to...

_____

_____

_____

_____

_____

Take a moment to pray what you have written, in the Name of Jesus. Allow Him to lead you back to Thanksgiving, Adoration, further Confession, or more Supplication/Intercession.

Non-Linear Prayer: Thanksgiving-Initiated Prayer Graph

If you are more visual or non-linear, use the chart below to write out your prayer points.

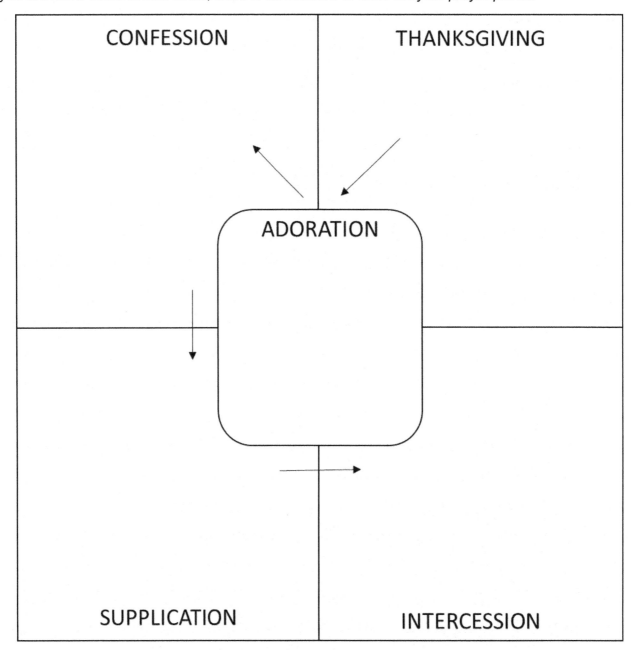

Week Twenty-Two

Week Of:

PRAYER STUDY

Read the Prayer: *Psalm 72*

Does the person praying in this Scripture use words of adoration for the Lord? If so, what are they?

_____

_____

_____

_____

_____

Does the person praying in this Scripture confess their sin? If not, does there seem to be an immaturity in their prayer where they needed to grow or a situation in their life that would warrant confession?

_____

_____

_____

_____

_____

Does the person praying in Scripture offer thanksgiving to God? If there is ample information about their life in the Bible, are there things in their story for which they should've been thankful?

_____

_____

_____

_____

_____

What, if any, are the requests they are making to God for themselves?

_____

_____

_____

_____

_____

What, if any, are the requests they are making on behalf of others?

_____

_____

_____

_____

_____

Your Prayer: The Adoration- Initiated Prayer

Think of an aspect of God's character. [Feel free to use phrases of adoration from Scripture]

Lord, you are...

_____

_____

_____

_____

_____

How do you or in what ways have you fallen short of that perfect character you mentioned in the adoration section?

I confess that...

_____

_____

_____

_____

_____

In light of this fallibility in you, where are you asking the Lord to grow you? For which brother or sister in Christ might you also pray to grow in this area of fallibility?

Lord, I ask you to...

_____

_____

_____

_____

_____

In what ways can you give thanksgiving to God in relation to all of this?

Lord, I ask you to...

_____

_____

_____

_____

_____

Take a moment to pray what you have written, in the Name of Jesus. Allow Him to lead you back to Adoration, further Confession, more Supplication/Intercession, and Thanksgiving.

Non-Linear Prayer: Adoration-Initiated Prayer Graph

If you are more visual or non-linear, use the chart below to write out your prayer points.

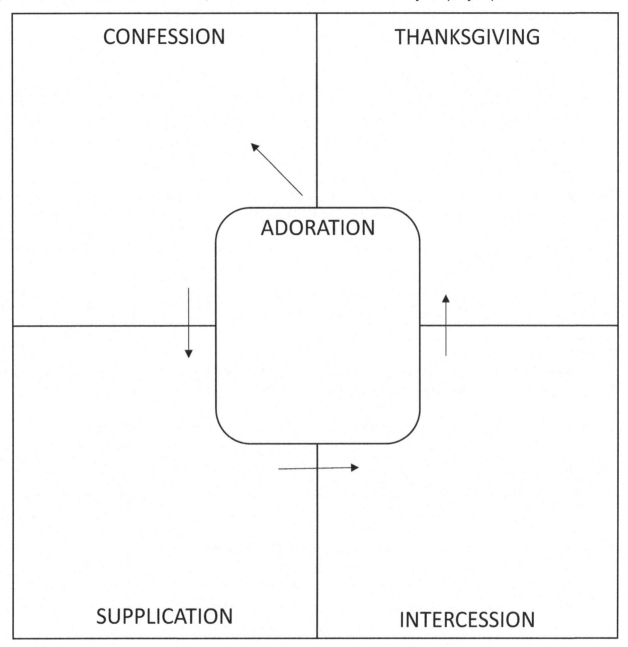

Week Twenty-Three

Week Of:

PRAYER STUDY

Read the Prayer: *Psalm 59*

Does the person praying in this Scripture use words of adoration for the Lord? If so, what are they?

_____

_____

_____

_____

_____

Does the person praying in this Scripture confess their sin? If not, does there seem to be an immaturity in their prayer where they needed to grow or a situation in their life that would warrant confession?

_____

_____

_____

_____

_____

Does the person praying in Scripture offer thanksgiving to God? If there is ample information about their life in the Bible, are there things in their story for which they should've been thankful?

_____

_____

_____

_____

_____

What, if any, are the requests they are making to God for themselves?

_____

_____

_____

_____

_____

What, if any, are the requests they are making on behalf of others?

_____

_____

_____

_____

_____

Your Prayer: The Confession- Initiated Prayer

Currently, where do you sense you are falling short of the glory of God? (Romans 3:23)

Lord, I confess...

_____

_____

_____

_____

_____

What does God's perfect character look like in contrast to your falling short?

But Lord, Your Word says that You are...

_____

_____

_____

_____

_____

What thanksgiving might you offer to God in regard to His mercy toward you or His offer of redemption in Christ or His patience with you? How has He specifically exhibited those things?

I thank you that...

_____

_____

_____

_____

_____

In what ways can you ask Him to grow you in grace? In what ways can you pray for particular unbelievers to recognize their own sin and trust in Christ alone?

Lord, I ask you to...

_____

_____

_____

_____

_____

Take a moment to pray what you have written, in the Name of Jesus. Allow Him to lead you back to further Confession, Adoration, Thanksgiving, and more Supplication/Intercession.

Non-Linear Prayer: Confession-Initiated Prayer Graph

If you are more visual or non-linear, use the chart below to write out your prayer points.

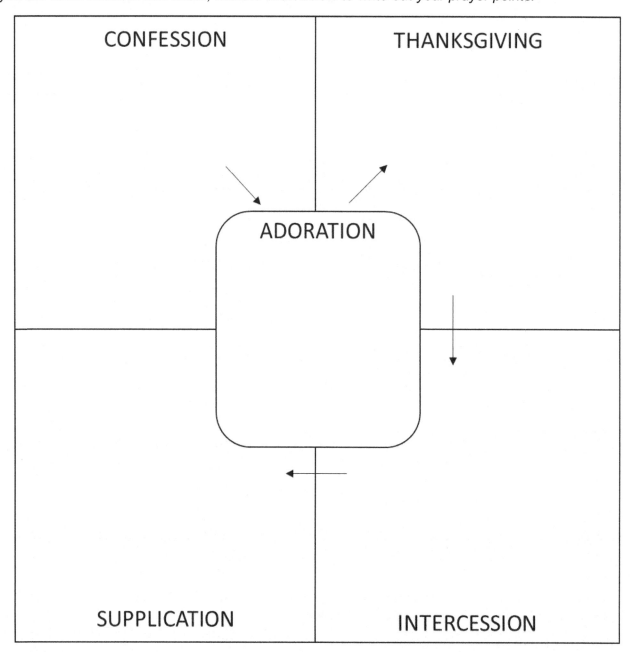

Week Twenty-Four

Week Of:

PRAYER STUDY

Read the Prayer: *Psalm 8*

Does the person praying in this Scripture use words of adoration for the Lord? If so, what are they?

_____

_____

_____

_____

_____

Does the person praying in this Scripture confess their sin? If not, does there seem to be an immaturity in their prayer where they needed to grow or a situation in their life that would warrant confession?

_____

_____

_____

_____

_____

Does the person praying in Scripture offer thanksgiving to God? If there is ample information about their life in the Bible, are there things in their story for which they should've been thankful?

_____

_____

_____

_____

_____

What, if any, are the requests they are making to God for themselves?

_____

_____

_____

_____

_____

What, if any, are the requests they are making on behalf of others?

_____

_____

_____

_____

_____

Your Prayer: The Supplication/Intersession- Initiated Prayer

What is the most pressing need you or someone else is struggling with?

Lord, I ask...

_____

_____

_____

_____

_____

How might you thank God for ways He has answered your prayers in the past?

Thank you for...

_____

_____

_____

_____

_____

What character of God do you need to be reminded of in light of your supplication/intercession request?

You have shown us in Your Word that You are...

_____

_____

_____

_____

_____

What might you need to confess in regard to all of this? Is there an attitude of doubt that the Lord will do and be all He has said He will do and be, etc?

Forgive me...

_____

_____

_____

_____

_____

Take a moment to pray what you have written, in the Name of Jesus. Allow Him to lead you back to Supplication/Intercession, Thanksgiving, Adoration, and further Confession.

Non-Linear Prayer: Supplication/Intercession-Initiated Prayer Graph

If you are more visual or non-linear, use the chart below to write out your prayer points.

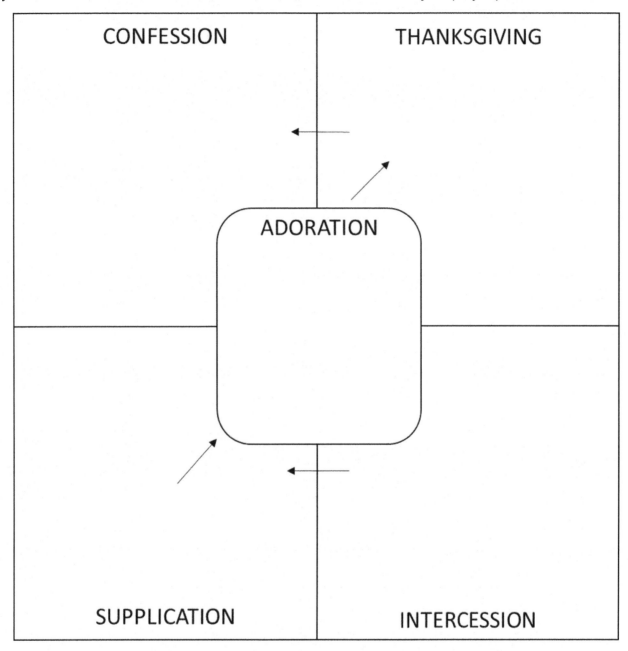

Week Twenty-Five

Week Of:

PRAYER STUDY

Read the Prayer: *Psalm 28*

Does the person praying in this Scripture use words of adoration for the Lord? If so, what are they?

_____

_____

_____

_____

_____

Does the person praying in this Scripture confess their sin? If not, does there seem to be an immaturity in their prayer where they needed to grow or a situation in their life that would warrant confession?

_____

_____

_____

_____

_____

Does the person praying in Scripture offer thanksgiving to God? If there is ample information about their life in the Bible, are there things in their story for which they should've been thankful?

_____

_____

_____

_____

_____

What, if any, are the requests they are making to God for themselves?

_____

_____

_____

_____

_____

What, if any, are the requests they are making on behalf of others?

_____

_____

_____

_____

_____

Your Prayer: The Thanksgiving- Initiated Prayer

What is something for which you are thankful? (Write it in the form of a prayer)

Dear Lord, thank you...

_____

_____

_____

_____

_____

What aspect of God's character did He show through what He provided?

Lord, you are...

_____

_____

_____

_____

_____

In light of God's character and His provision, what about your actions or attitude of your own heart do you need to confess?

Lord, forgive me...

_____

_____

_____

_____

_____

What do you need to ask Him to do within you or for you or for others in light of all of the above?

Lord, I ask you to...

_____

_____

_____

_____

_____

Take a moment to pray what you have written, in the Name of Jesus. Allow Him to lead you back to Thanksgiving, Adoration, further Confession, or more Supplication/Intercession.

Non-Linear Prayer: Thanksgiving-Initiated Prayer Graph

If you are more visual or non-linear, use the chart below to write out your prayer points.

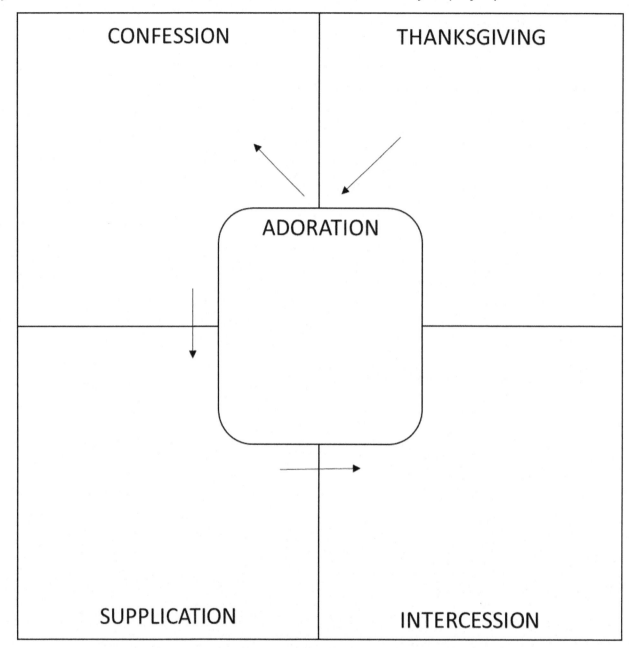

Week Twenty-Six

Week Of:

PRAYER STUDY

Read the Prayer: *Psalm 31*

Does the person praying in this Scripture use words of adoration for the Lord? If so, what are they?

_____

_____

_____

_____

_____

Does the person praying in this Scripture confess their sin? If not, does there seem to be an immaturity in their prayer where they needed to grow or a situation in their life that would warrant confession?

_____

_____

_____

_____

_____

Does the person praying in Scripture offer thanksgiving to God? If there is ample information about their life in the Bible, are there things in their story for which they should've been thankful?

_____

_____

_____

_____

_____

What, if any, are the requests they are making to God for themselves?

_____

_____

_____

_____

_____

What, if any, are the requests they are making on behalf of others?

_____

_____

_____

_____

_____

Your Prayer: The Adoration- Initiated Prayer

Think of an aspect of God's character. [Feel free to use phrases of adoration from Scripture]

Lord, you are...

_____
_____
_____
_____
_____

How do you or in what ways have you fallen short of that perfect character you mentioned in the adoration section?

I confess that...

_____
_____
_____
_____
_____

In light of this fallibility in you, where are you asking the Lord to grow you? For which brother or sister in Christ might you also pray to grow in this area of fallibility?

Lord, I ask you to...

_____
_____
_____
_____
_____

In what ways can you give thanksgiving to God in relation to all of this?

Lord, I ask you to...

_____
_____
_____
_____
_____

Take a moment to pray what you have written, in the Name of Jesus. Allow Him to lead you back to Adoration, further Confession, more Supplication/Intercession, and Thanksgiving.

Non-Linear Prayer: Adoration-Initiated Prayer Graph

If you are more visual or non-linear, use the chart below to write out your prayer points.

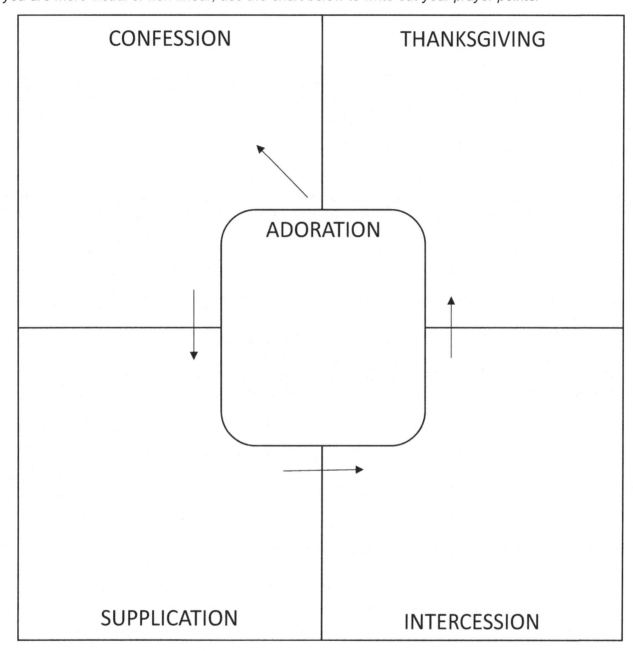

Week Twenty-Seven

Week Of:

PRAYER STUDY

Read the Prayer: *Psalm 56*

Does the person praying in this Scripture use words of adoration for the Lord? If so, what are they?

_____

_____

_____

_____

_____

Does the person praying in this Scripture confess their sin? If not, does there seem to be an immaturity in their prayer where they needed to grow or a situation in their life that would warrant confession?

_____

_____

_____

_____

_____

Does the person praying in Scripture offer thanksgiving to God? If there is ample information about their life in the Bible, are there things in their story for which they should've been thankful?

_____

_____

_____

_____

_____

What, if any, are the requests they are making to God for themselves?

_____

_____

_____

_____

_____

What, if any, are the requests they are making on behalf of others?

_____

_____

_____

_____

_____

Your Prayer: The Confession- Initiated Prayer

Currently, where do you sense you are falling short of the glory of God? (Romans 3:23)

Lord, I confess...

_____

_____

_____

_____

_____

What does God's perfect character look like in contrast to your falling short?

But Lord, Your Word says that You are...

_____

_____

_____

_____

_____

What thanksgiving might you offer to God in regard to His mercy toward you or His offer of redemption in Christ or His patience with you? How has He specifically exhibited those things?

I thank you that...

_____

_____

_____

_____

_____

In what ways can you ask Him to grow you in grace? In what ways can you pray for particular unbelievers to recognize their own sin and trust in Christ alone?

Lord, I ask you to...

_____

_____

_____

_____

_____

Take a moment to pray what you have written, in the Name of Jesus. Allow Him to lead you back to further Confession, Adoration, Thanksgiving, and more Supplication/Intercession.

Non-Linear Prayer: Confession-Initiated Prayer Graph

If you are more visual or non-linear, use the chart below to write out your prayer points.

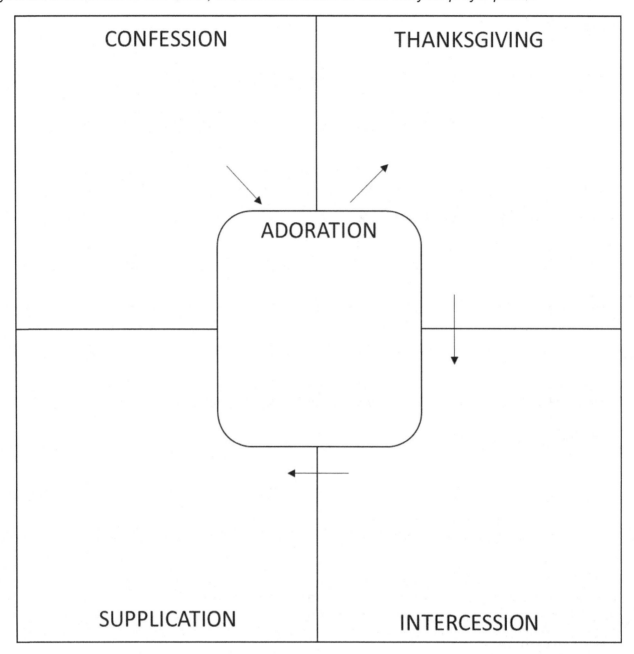

Week Twenty-Eight

Week Of:

PRAYER STUDY

Read the Prayer: *Psalm 145*

Does the person praying in this Scripture use words of adoration for the Lord? If so, what are they?

_____

_____

_____

_____

_____

Does the person praying in this Scripture confess their sin? If not, does there seem to be an immaturity in their prayer where they needed to grow or a situation in their life that would warrant confession?

_____

_____

_____

_____

_____

Does the person praying in Scripture offer thanksgiving to God? If there is ample information about their life in the Bible, are there things in their story for which they should've been thankful?

_____

_____

_____

_____

_____

What, if any, are the requests they are making to God for themselves?

_____

_____

_____

_____

_____

What, if any, are the requests they are making on behalf of others?

_____

_____

_____

_____

_____

Your Prayer: The Supplication/Intersession- Initiated Prayer

What is the most pressing need you or someone else is struggling with?

Lord, I ask...

_____

_____

_____

_____

_____

How might you thank God for ways He has answered your prayers in the past?

Thank you for...

_____

_____

_____

_____

_____

What character of God do you need to be reminded of in light of your supplication/intercession request?

You have shown us in Your Word that You are...

_____

_____

_____

_____

_____

What might you need to confess in regard to all of this? Is there an attitude of doubt that the Lord will do and be all He has said He will do and be, etc?

Forgive me...

_____

_____

_____

_____

_____

Take a moment to pray what you have written, in the Name of Jesus. Allow Him to lead you back to Supplication/Intercession, Thanksgiving, Adoration, and further Confession.

Non-Linear Prayer: Supplication/Intercession-Initiated Prayer Graph

If you are more visual or non-linear, use the chart below to write out your prayer points.

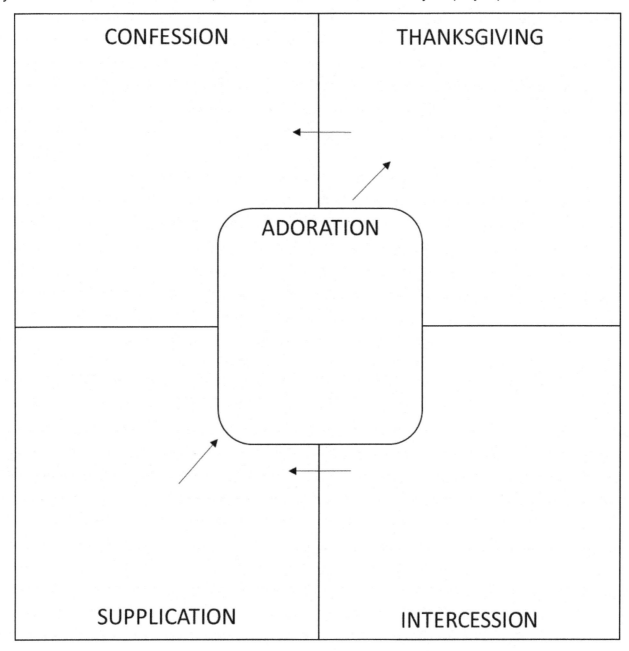

Week Twenty-Nine

Week Of:

PRAYER STUDY

Read the Prayer: *Psalm 141*

Does the person praying in this Scripture use words of adoration for the Lord? If so, what are they?

_____

_____

_____

_____

_____

Does the person praying in this Scripture confess their sin? If not, does there seem to be an immaturity in their prayer where they needed to grow or a situation in their life that would warrant confession?

_____

_____

_____

_____

_____

Does the person praying in Scripture offer thanksgiving to God? If there is ample information about their life in the Bible, are there things in their story for which they should've been thankful?

_____

_____

_____

_____

_____

What, if any, are the requests they are making to God for themselves?

_____

_____

_____

_____

_____

What, if any, are the requests they are making on behalf of others?

_____

_____

_____

_____

_____

Your Prayer: The Thanksgiving- Initiated Prayer

What is something for which you are thankful? (Write it in the form of a prayer)

Dear Lord, thank you...

_____
_____
_____
_____
_____

What aspect of God's character did He show through what He provided?

Lord, you are...

_____
_____
_____
_____
_____

In light of God's character and His provision, what about your actions or attitude of your own heart do you need to confess?

Lord, forgive me...

_____
_____
_____
_____
_____

What do you need to ask Him to do within you or for you or for others in light of all of the above?

Lord, I ask you to...

_____
_____
_____
_____
_____

Take a moment to pray what you have written, in the Name of Jesus. Allow Him to lead you back to Thanksgiving, Adoration, further Confession, or more Supplication/Intercession.

Non-Linear Prayer: Thanksgiving-Initiated Prayer Graph

If you are more visual or non-linear, use the chart below to write out your prayer points.

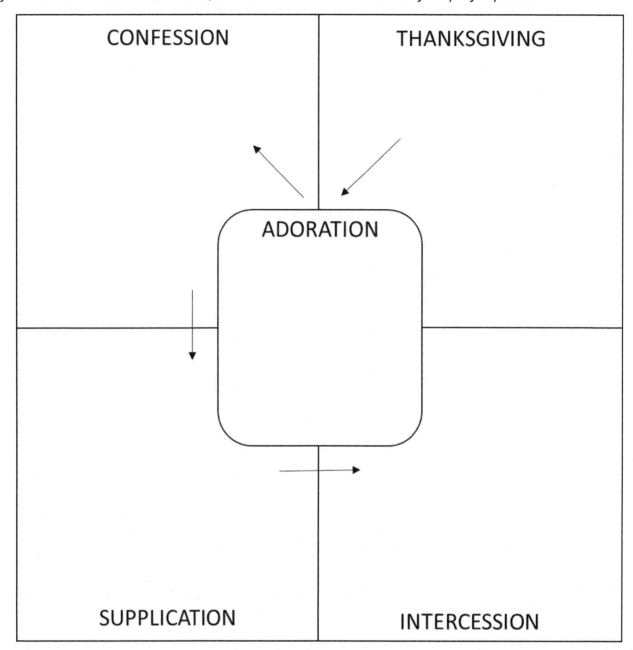

Week Thirty

PRAYER STUDY

Read the Prayer: *Psalm 25*

Does the person praying in this Scripture use words of adoration for the Lord? If so, what are they?

_____

_____

_____

_____

_____

Does the person praying in this Scripture confess their sin? If not, does there seem to be an immaturity in their prayer where they needed to grow or a situation in their life that would warrant confession?

_____

_____

_____

_____

_____

Does the person praying in Scripture offer thanksgiving to God? If there is ample information about their life in the Bible, are there things in their story for which they should've been thankful?

_____

_____

_____

_____

_____

What, if any, are the requests they are making to God for themselves?

_____

_____

_____

_____

_____

What, if any, are the requests they are making on behalf of others?

_____

_____

_____

_____

_____

Your Prayer: The Adoration- Initiated Prayer

Think of an aspect of God's character. [Feel free to use phrases of adoration from Scripture]

Lord, you are...

_____

_____

_____

_____

_____

How do you or in what ways have you fallen short of that perfect character you mentioned in the adoration section?

I confess that...

_____

_____

_____

_____

_____

In light of this fallibility in you, where are you asking the Lord to grow you? For which brother or sister in Christ might you also pray to grow in this area of fallibility?

Lord, I ask you to...

_____

_____

_____

_____

_____

In what ways can you give thanksgiving to God in relation to all of this?

Lord, I ask you to...

_____

_____

_____

_____

_____

Take a moment to pray what you have written, in the Name of Jesus. Allow Him to lead you back to Adoration, further Confession, more Supplication/Intercession, and Thanksgiving.

Non-Linear Prayer: Adoration-Initiated Prayer Graph

If you are more visual or non-linear, use the chart below to write out your prayer points.

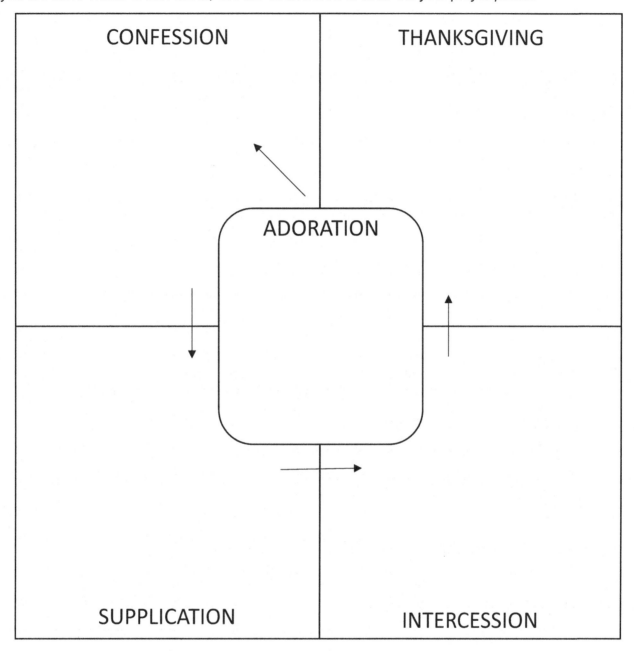

Week Thirty-One

Week Of:

PRAYER STUDY

Read the Prayer: *Psalm 83*

Does the person praying in this Scripture use words of adoration for the Lord? If so, what are they?

_____

_____

_____

_____

_____

Does the person praying in this Scripture confess their sin? If not, does there seem to be an immaturity in their prayer where they needed to grow or a situation in their life that would warrant confession?

_____

_____

_____

_____

Does the person praying in Scripture offer thanksgiving to God? If there is ample information about their life in the Bible, are there things in their story for which they should've been thankful?

_____

_____

_____

_____

_____

What, if any, are the requests they are making to God for themselves?

_____

_____

_____

_____

_____

What, if any, are the requests they are making on behalf of others?

_____

_____

_____

_____

_____

Your Prayer: The Confession- Initiated Prayer

Currently, where do you sense you are falling short of the glory of God? (Romans 3:23)

Lord, I confess...

_____

_____

_____

_____

_____

What does God's perfect character look like in contrast to your falling short?

But Lord, Your Word says that You are...

_____

_____

_____

_____

_____

What thanksgiving might you offer to God in regard to His mercy toward you or His offer of redemption in Christ or His patience with you? How has He specifically exhibited those things?

I thank you that...

_____

_____

_____

_____

_____

In what ways can you ask Him to grow you in grace? In what ways can you pray for particular unbelievers to recognize their own sin and trust in Christ alone?

Lord, I ask you to...

_____

_____

_____

_____

_____

Take a moment to pray what you have written, in the Name of Jesus. Allow Him to lead you back to further Confession, Adoration, Thanksgiving, and more Supplication/Intercession.

Non-Linear Prayer: Confession-Initiated Prayer Graph

If you are more visual or non-linear, use the chart below to write out your prayer points.

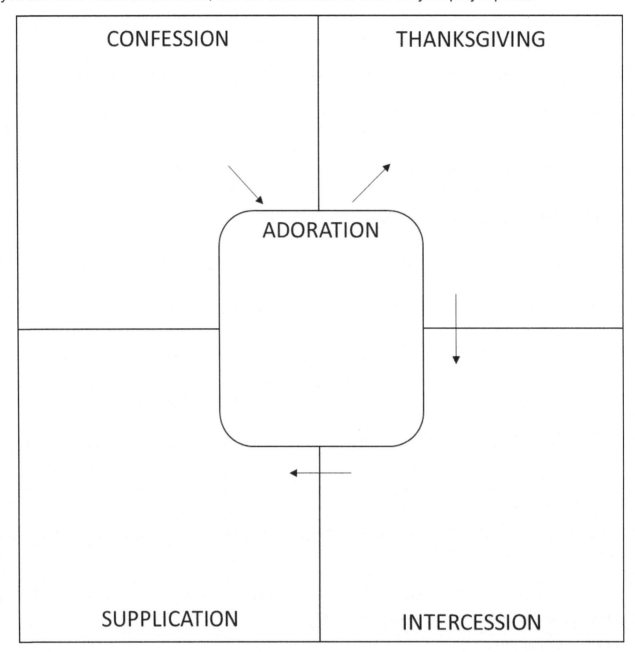

Week Thirty-Two

Week Of:

PRAYER STUDY

Read the Prayer: *Jeremiah 12:1-6*

Does the person praying in this Scripture use words of adoration for the Lord? If so, what are they?

_____

_____

_____

_____

Does the person praying in this Scripture confess their sin? If not, does there seem to be an immaturity in their prayer where they needed to grow or a situation in their life that would warrant confession?

_____

_____

_____

_____

Does the person praying in Scripture offer thanksgiving to God? If there is ample information about their life in the Bible, are there things in their story for which they should've been thankful?

_____

_____

_____

_____

What, if any, are the requests they are making to God for themselves?

_____

_____

_____

_____

What, if any, are the requests they are making on behalf of others?

_____

_____

_____

_____

Your Prayer: The Supplication/Intersession- Initiated Prayer

What is the most pressing need you or someone else is struggling with?

Lord, I ask...

_____
_____
_____
_____
_____

How might you thank God for ways He has answered your prayers in the past?

Thank you for...

_____
_____
_____
_____
_____

What character of God do you need to be reminded of in light of your supplication/intercession request?

You have shown us in Your Word that You are...

_____
_____
_____
_____
_____

What might you need to confess in regard to all of this? Is there an attitude of doubt that the Lord will do and be all He has said He will do and be, etc?

Forgive me...

_____
_____
_____
_____
_____

Take a moment to pray what you have written, in the Name of Jesus. Allow Him to lead you back to Supplication/Intercession, Thanksgiving, Adoration, and further Confession.

Non-Linear Prayer: Supplication/Intercession-Initiated Prayer Graph

If you are more visual or non-linear, use the chart below to write out your prayer points.

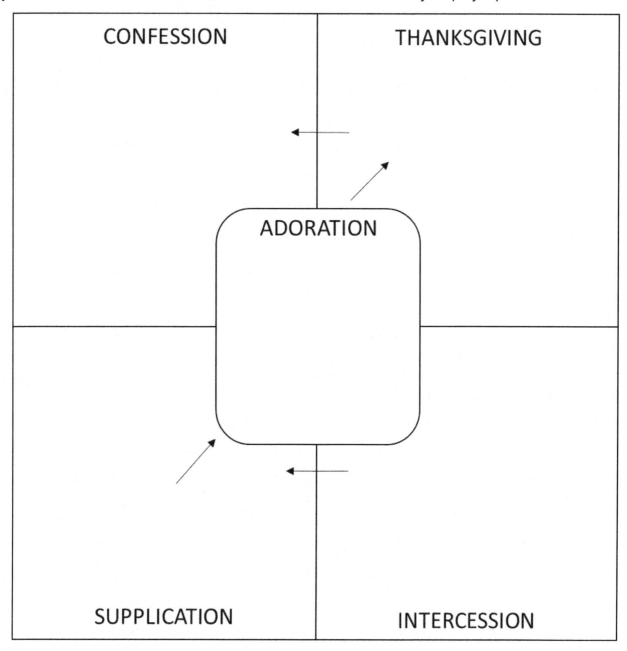

Week Thirty-Three

Week Of:

PRAYER STUDY

Read the Prayer: *Daniel 9:4-19*

Does the person praying in this Scripture use words of adoration for the Lord? If so, what are they?

_____

_____

_____

_____

_____

Does the person praying in this Scripture confess their sin? If not, does there seem to be an immaturity in their prayer where they needed to grow or a situation in their life that would warrant confession?

_____

_____

_____

_____

_____

Does the person praying in Scripture offer thanksgiving to God? If there is ample information about their life in the Bible, are there things in their story for which they should've been thankful?

_____

_____

_____

_____

_____

What, if any, are the requests they are making to God for themselves?

_____

_____

_____

_____

_____

What, if any, are the requests they are making on behalf of others?

_____

_____

_____

_____

_____

Your Prayer: The Thanksgiving- Initiated Prayer

What is something for which you are thankful? (Write it in the form of a prayer)

Dear Lord, thank you…

_____

_____

_____

_____

_____

What aspect of God's character did He show through what He provided?

Lord, you are…

_____

_____

_____

_____

_____

In light of God's character and His provision, what about your actions or attitude of your own heart do you need to confess?

Lord, forgive me…

_____

_____

_____

_____

_____

What do you need to ask Him to do within you or for you or for others in light of all of the above?

Lord, I ask you to…

_____

_____

_____

_____

_____

Take a moment to pray what you have written, in the Name of Jesus. Allow Him to lead you back to Thanksgiving, Adoration, further Confession, or more Supplication/Intercession.

Non-Linear Prayer: Thanksgiving-Initiated Prayer Graph

If you are more visual or non-linear, use the chart below to write out your prayer points.

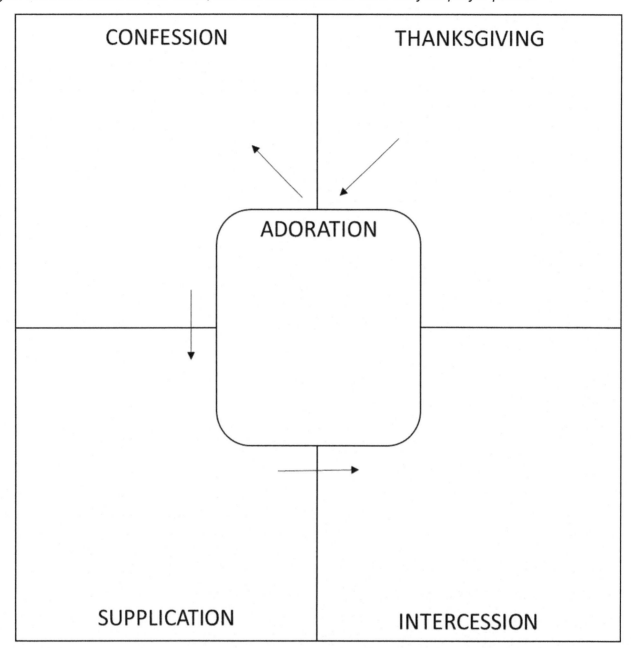

Week Thirty-Four

Week Of:

PRAYER STUDY

Read the Prayer: *Habakkuk 1:12-17*

Does the person praying in this Scripture use words of adoration for the Lord? If so, what are they?

_____

_____

_____

_____

_____

Does the person praying in this Scripture confess their sin? If not, does there seem to be an immaturity in their prayer where they needed to grow or a situation in their life that would warrant confession?

_____

_____

_____

_____

_____

Does the person praying in Scripture offer thanksgiving to God? If there is ample information about their life in the Bible, are there things in their story for which they should've been thankful?

_____

_____

_____

_____

_____

What, if any, are the requests they are making to God for themselves?

_____

_____

_____

_____

What, if any, are the requests they are making on behalf of others?

_____

_____

_____

_____

Your Prayer: The Adoration- Initiated Prayer

Think of an aspect of God's character. [Feel free to use phrases of adoration from Scripture]

Lord, you are...

_____
_____
_____
_____
_____

How do you or in what ways have you fallen short of that perfect character you mentioned in the adoration section?

I confess that...

_____
_____
_____
_____
_____

In light of this fallibility in you, where are you asking the Lord to grow you? For which brother or sister in Christ might you also pray to grow in this area of fallibility?

Lord, I ask you to...

_____
_____
_____
_____
_____

In what ways can you give thanksgiving to God in relation to all of this?

Lord, I ask you to...

_____
_____
_____
_____
_____

Take a moment to pray what you have written, in the Name of Jesus. Allow Him to lead you back to Adoration, further Confession, more Supplication/Intercession, and Thanksgiving.

Non-Linear Prayer: Adoration-Initiated Prayer Graph

If you are more visual or non-linear, use the chart below to write out your prayer points.

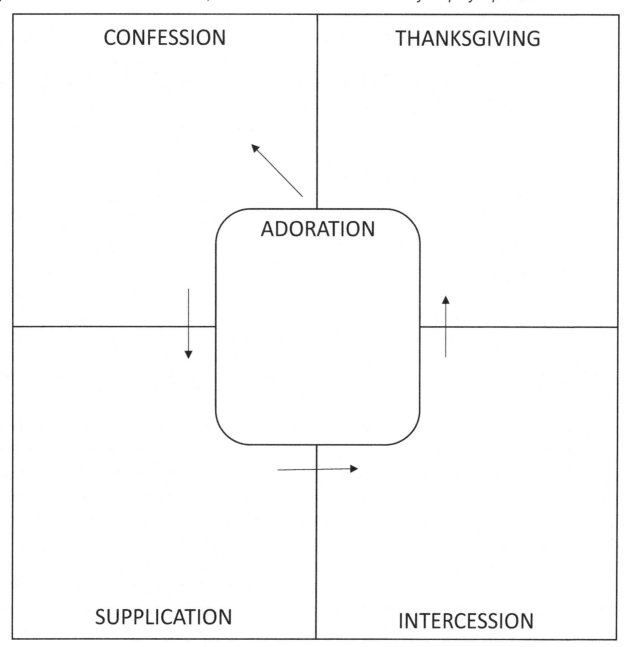

Week Thirty-Five

Week Of:

PRAYER STUDY

Read the Prayer: *Psalm 35*

Does the person praying in this Scripture use words of adoration for the Lord? If so, what are they?

_____

_____

_____

_____

_____

Does the person praying in this Scripture confess their sin? If not, does there seem to be an immaturity in their prayer where they needed to grow or a situation in their life that would warrant confession?

_____

_____

_____

_____

_____

Does the person praying in Scripture offer thanksgiving to God? If there is ample information about their life in the Bible, are there things in their story for which they should've been thankful?

_____

_____

_____

_____

_____

What, if any, are the requests they are making to God for themselves?

_____

_____

_____

_____

_____

What, if any, are the requests they are making on behalf of others?

_____

_____

_____

_____

_____

Your Prayer: The Confession- Initiated Prayer

Currently, where do you sense you are falling short of the glory of God? (Romans 3:23)

Lord, I confess...

_____

_____

_____

_____

_____

What does God's perfect character look like in contrast to your falling short?

But Lord, Your Word says that You are...

_____

_____

_____

_____

_____

What thanksgiving might you offer to God in regard to His mercy toward you or His offer of redemption in Christ or His patience with you? How has He specifically exhibited those things?

I thank you that...

_____

_____

_____

_____

_____

In what ways can you ask Him to grow you in grace? In what ways can you pray for particular unbelievers to recognize their own sin and trust in Christ alone?

Lord, I ask you to...

_____

_____

_____

_____

_____

Take a moment to pray what you have written, in the Name of Jesus. Allow Him to lead you back to further Confession, Adoration, Thanksgiving, and more Supplication/Intercession.

Non-Linear Prayer: Confession-Initiated Prayer Graph

If you are more visual or non-linear, use the chart below to write out your prayer points.

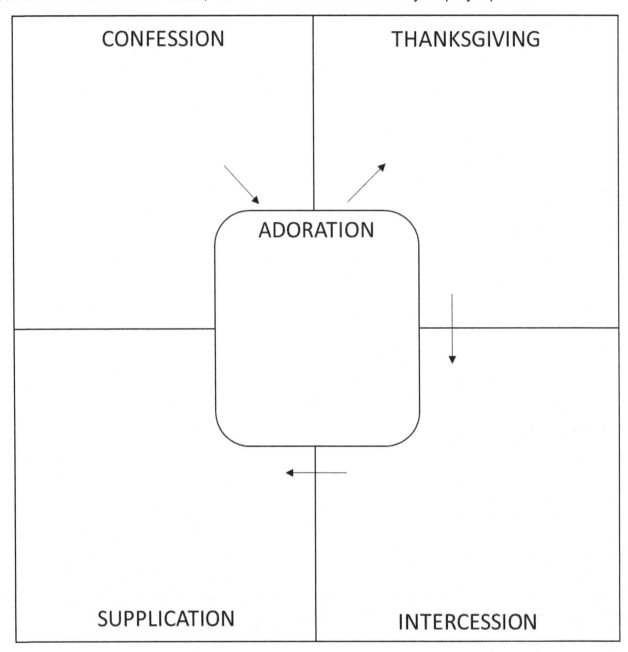

Week Thirty-Six   **Week Of:**

PRAYER STUDY

Read the Prayer: *Psalm 39*

Does the person praying in this Scripture use words of adoration for the Lord? If so, what are they?

_____

_____

_____

_____

_____

Does the person praying in this Scripture confess their sin? If not, does there seem to be an immaturity in their prayer where they needed to grow or a situation in their life that would warrant confession?

_____

_____

_____

_____

_____

Does the person praying in Scripture offer thanksgiving to God? If there is ample information about their life in the Bible, are there things in their story for which they should've been thankful?

_____

_____

_____

_____

_____

What, if any, are the requests they are making to God for themselves?

_____

_____

_____

_____

_____

What, if any, are the requests they are making on behalf of others?

_____

_____

_____

_____

_____

Your Prayer: The Supplication/Intersession- Initiated Prayer

What is the most pressing need you or someone else is struggling with?

Lord, I ask...

_____

_____

_____

_____

_____

How might you thank God for ways He has answered your prayers in the past?

Thank you for...

_____

_____

_____

_____

_____

What character of God do you need to be reminded of in light of your supplication/intercession request?

You have shown us in Your Word that You are...

_____

_____

_____

_____

_____

What might you need to confess in regard to all of this? Is there an attitude of doubt that the Lord will do and be all He has said He will do and be, etc?

Forgive me...

_____

_____

_____

_____

_____

Take a moment to pray what you have written, in the Name of Jesus. Allow Him to lead you back to Supplication/Intercession, Thanksgiving, Adoration, and further Confession.

Non-Linear Prayer: Supplication/Intercession-Initiated Prayer Graph

If you are more visual or non-linear, use the chart below to write out your prayer points.

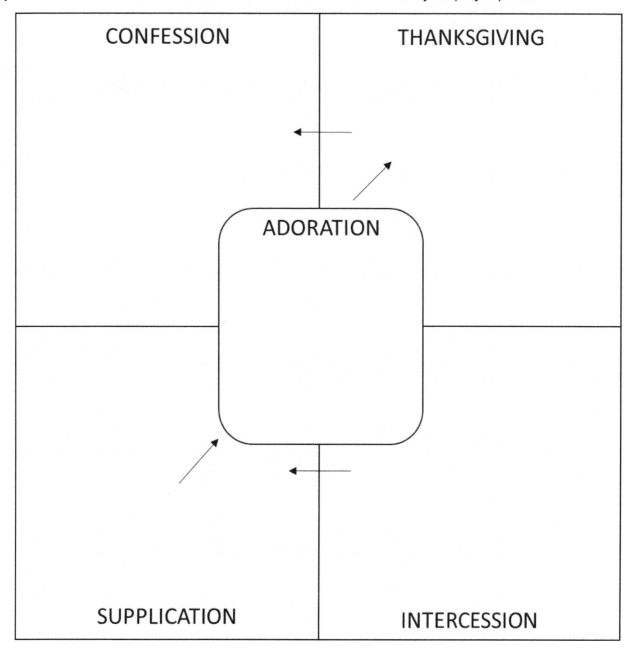

Week Thirty-Seven

Week Of:

PRAYER STUDY

Read the Prayer: *Psalm 102*

Does the person praying in this Scripture use words of adoration for the Lord? If so, what are they?

_____

_____

_____

_____

_____

Does the person praying in this Scripture confess their sin? If not, does there seem to be an immaturity in their prayer where they needed to grow or a situation in their life that would warrant confession?

_____

_____

_____

_____

_____

Does the person praying in Scripture offer thanksgiving to God? If there is ample information about their life in the Bible, are there things in their story for which they should've been thankful?

_____

_____

_____

_____

_____

What, if any, are the requests they are making to God for themselves?

_____

_____

_____

_____

_____

What, if any, are the requests they are making on behalf of others?

_____

_____

_____

_____

_____

Your Prayer: The Thanksgiving- Initiated Prayer

What is something for which you are thankful? (Write it in the form of a prayer)

Dear Lord, thank you…

_____

_____

_____

_____

_____

What aspect of God's character did He show through what He provided?

Lord, you are…

_____

_____

_____

_____

_____

In light of God's character and His provision, what about your actions or attitude of your own heart do you need to confess?

Lord, forgive me…

_____

_____

_____

_____

_____

What do you need to ask Him to do within you or for you or for others in light of all of the above?

Lord, I ask you to…

_____

_____

_____

_____

_____

Take a moment to pray what you have written, in the Name of Jesus. Allow Him to lead you back to Thanksgiving, Adoration, further Confession, or more Supplication/Intercession.

Non-Linear Prayer: Thanksgiving-Initiated Prayer Graph

If you are more visual or non-linear, use the chart below to write out your prayer points.

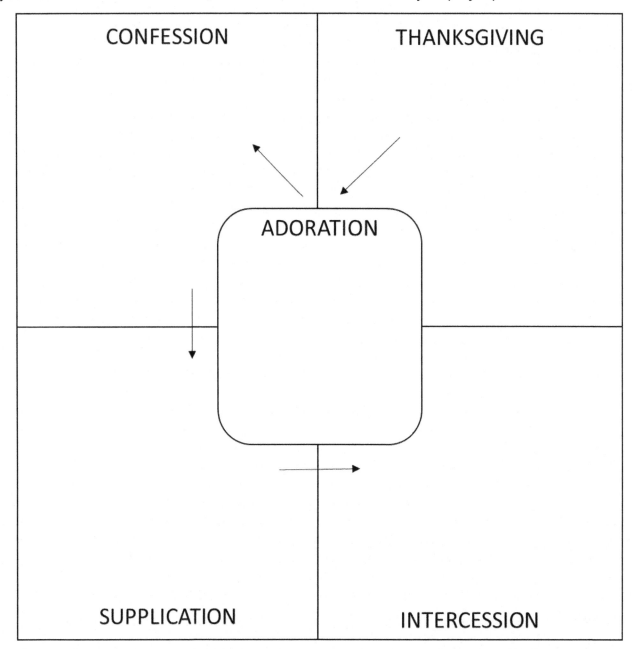

Week Thirty-Eight

Week Of:

PRAYER STUDY

Read the Prayer: *Psalm 55*

Does the person praying in this Scripture use words of adoration for the Lord? If so, what are they?

_____

_____

_____

_____

_____

Does the person praying in this Scripture confess their sin? If not, does there seem to be an immaturity in their prayer where they needed to grow or a situation in their life that would warrant confession?

_____

_____

_____

_____

_____

Does the person praying in Scripture offer thanksgiving to God? If there is ample information about their life in the Bible, are there things in their story for which they should've been thankful?

_____

_____

_____

_____

_____

What, if any, are the requests they are making to God for themselves?

_____

_____

_____

_____

What, if any, are the requests they are making on behalf of others?

_____

_____

_____

_____

Your Prayer: The Adoration- Initiated Prayer

Think of an aspect of God's character. [Feel free to use phrases of adoration from Scripture]

Lord, you are…

_____
_____
_____
_____
_____

How do you or in what ways have you fallen short of that perfect character you mentioned in the adoration section?

I confess that…

_____
_____
_____
_____
_____

In light of this fallibility in you, where are you asking the Lord to grow you? For which brother or sister in Christ might you also pray to grow in this area of fallibility?

Lord, I ask you to…

_____
_____
_____
_____
_____

In what ways can you give thanksgiving to God in relation to all of this?

Lord, I ask you to…

_____
_____
_____
_____
_____

Take a moment to pray what you have written, in the Name of Jesus. Allow Him to lead you back to Adoration, further Confession, more Supplication/Intercession, and Thanksgiving.

Non-Linear Prayer: Adoration-Initiated Prayer Graph

If you are more visual or non-linear, use the chart below to write out your prayer points.

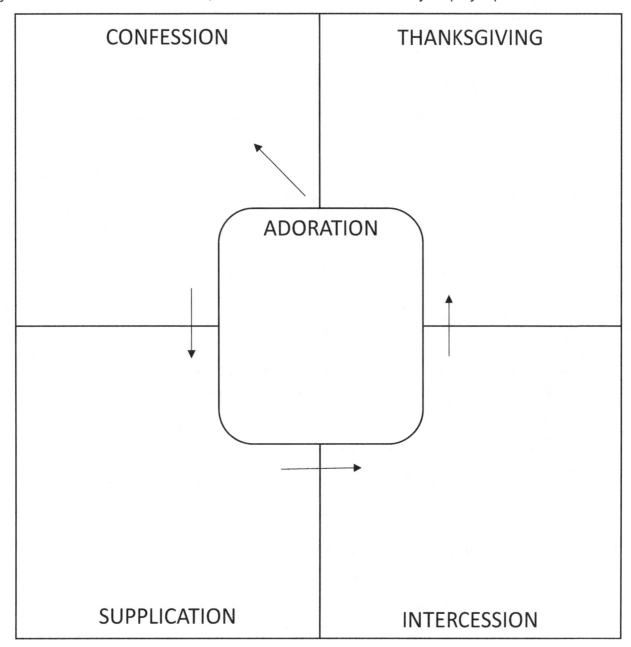

Week Thirty-Nine

Week Of:

PRAYER STUDY

Read the Prayer: *Psalm 21*

Does the person praying in this Scripture use words of adoration for the Lord? If so, what are they?

_____

_____

_____

_____

_____

Does the person praying in this Scripture confess their sin? If not, does there seem to be an immaturity in their prayer where they needed to grow or a situation in their life that would warrant confession?

_____

_____

_____

_____

_____

Does the person praying in Scripture offer thanksgiving to God? If there is ample information about their life in the Bible, are there things in their story for which they should've been thankful?

_____

_____

_____

_____

_____

What, if any, are the requests they are making to God for themselves?

_____

_____

_____

_____

_____

What, if any, are the requests they are making on behalf of others?

_____

_____

_____

_____

_____

Your Prayer: The Confession- Initiated Prayer

Currently, where do you sense you are falling short of the glory of God? (Romans 3:23)

Lord, I confess...

_____
_____
_____
_____
_____

What does God's perfect character look like in contrast to your falling short?

But Lord, Your Word says that You are...

_____
_____
_____
_____
_____

What thanksgiving might you offer to God in regard to His mercy toward you or His offer of redemption in Christ or His patience with you? How has He specifically exhibited those things?

I thank you that...

_____
_____
_____
_____
_____

In what ways can you ask Him to grow you in grace? In what ways can you pray for particular unbelievers to recognize their own sin and trust in Christ alone?

Lord, I ask you to...

_____
_____
_____
_____
_____

Take a moment to pray what you have written, in the Name of Jesus. Allow Him to lead you back to further Confession, Adoration, Thanksgiving, and more Supplication/Intercession.

Non-Linear Prayer: Confession-Initiated Prayer Graph

If you are more visual or non-linear, use the chart below to write out your prayer points.

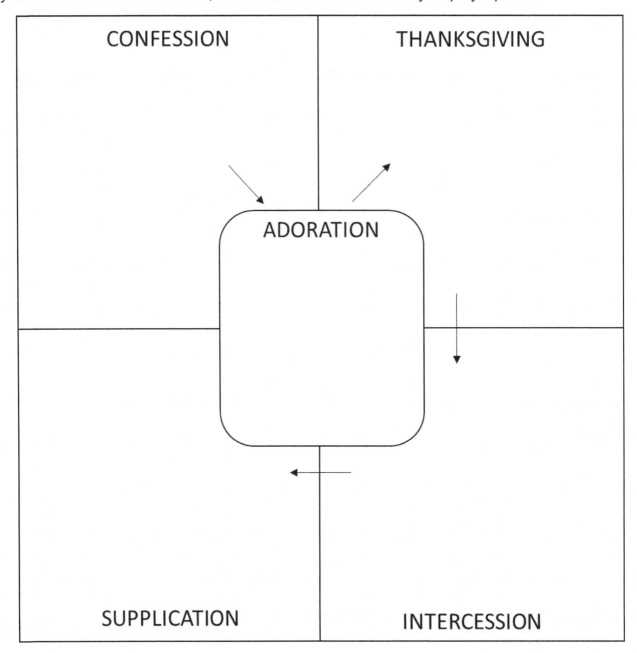

Week Forty

PRAYER STUDY

Read the Prayer: *Psalm 71*

Does the person praying in this Scripture use words of adoration for the Lord? If so, what are they?

_____

_____

_____

_____

_____

Does the person praying in this Scripture confess their sin? If not, does there seem to be an immaturity in their prayer where they needed to grow or a situation in their life that would warrant confession?

_____

_____

_____

_____

_____

Does the person praying in Scripture offer thanksgiving to God? If there is ample information about their life in the Bible, are there things in their story for which they should've been thankful?

_____

_____

_____

_____

_____

What, if any, are the requests they are making to God for themselves?

_____

_____

_____

_____

_____

What, if any, are the requests they are making on behalf of others?

_____

_____

_____

_____

_____

Your Prayer: The Supplication/Intersession- Initiated Prayer

What is the most pressing need you or someone else is struggling with?

Lord, I ask...

_____

_____

_____

_____

_____

How might you thank God for ways He has answered your prayers in the past?

Thank you for...

_____

_____

_____

_____

_____

What character of God do you need to be reminded of in light of your supplication/intercession request?

You have shown us in Your Word that You are...

_____

_____

_____

_____

_____

What might you need to confess in regard to all of this? Is there an attitude of doubt that the Lord will do and be all He has said He will do and be, etc?

Forgive me...

_____

_____

_____

_____

_____

Take a moment to pray what you have written, in the Name of Jesus. Allow Him to lead you back to Supplication/Intercession, Thanksgiving, Adoration, and further Confession.

Non-Linear Prayer: Supplication/Intercession-Initiated Prayer Graph

If you are more visual or non-linear, use the chart below to write out your prayer points.

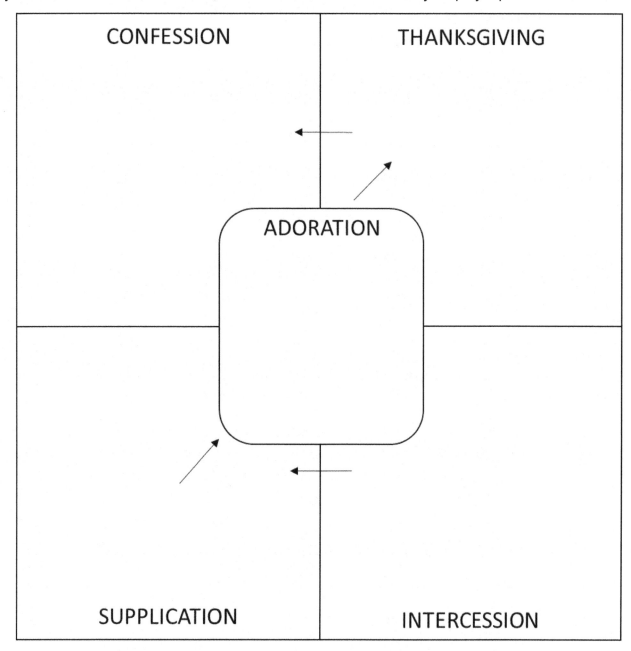

Week Forty-One

Week Of:

PRAYER STUDY

Read the Prayer: *Psalm 42*

Does the person praying in this Scripture use words of adoration for the Lord? If so, what are they?

_____

_____

_____

_____

_____

Does the person praying in this Scripture confess their sin? If not, does there seem to be an immaturity in their prayer where they needed to grow or a situation in their life that would warrant confession?

_____

_____

_____

_____

_____

Does the person praying in Scripture offer thanksgiving to God? If there is ample information about their life in the Bible, are there things in their story for which they should've been thankful?

_____

_____

_____

_____

_____

What, if any, are the requests they are making to God for themselves?

_____

_____

_____

_____

_____

What, if any, are the requests they are making on behalf of others?

_____

_____

_____

_____

_____

Your Prayer: The Thanksgiving- Initiated Prayer

What is something for which you are thankful? (Write it in the form of a prayer)

Dear Lord, thank you...

_____

_____

_____

_____

_____

What aspect of God's character did He show through what He provided?

Lord, you are...

_____

_____

_____

_____

_____

In light of God's character and His provision, what about your actions or attitude of your own heart do you need to confess?

Lord, forgive me...

_____

_____

_____

_____

_____

What do you need to ask Him to do within you or for you or for others in light of all of the above?

Lord, I ask you to...

_____

_____

_____

_____

_____

Take a moment to pray what you have written, in the Name of Jesus. Allow Him to lead you back to Thanksgiving, Adoration, further Confession, or more Supplication/Intercession.

Non-Linear Prayer: Thanksgiving-Initiated Prayer Graph

If you are more visual or non-linear, use the chart below to write out your prayer points.

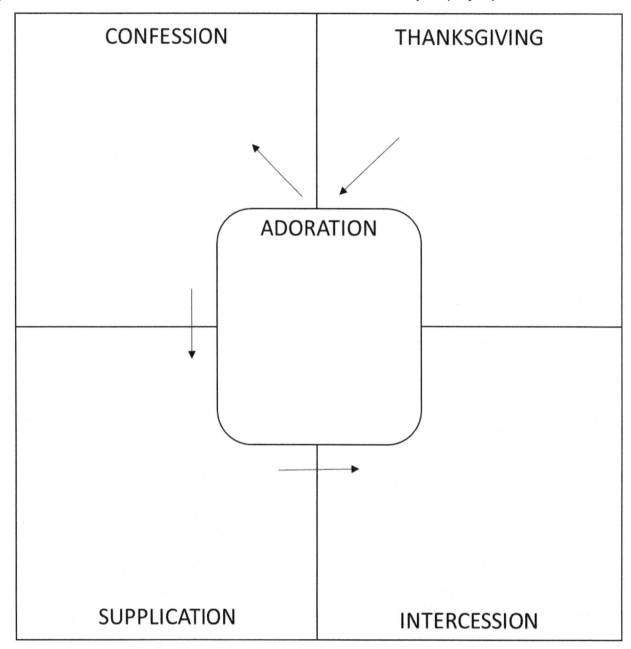

Week Forty-Two

Week Of:

PRAYER STUDY

Read the Prayer: *Psalm 54*

Does the person praying in this Scripture use words of adoration for the Lord? If so, what are they?

_____

_____

_____

_____

_____

Does the person praying in this Scripture confess their sin? If not, does there seem to be an immaturity in their prayer where they needed to grow or a situation in their life that would warrant confession?

_____

_____

_____

_____

_____

Does the person praying in Scripture offer thanksgiving to God? If there is ample information about their life in the Bible, are there things in their story for which they should've been thankful?

_____

_____

_____

_____

_____

What, if any, are the requests they are making to God for themselves?

_____

_____

_____

_____

_____

What, if any, are the requests they are making on behalf of others?

_____

_____

_____

_____

_____

Your Prayer: The Adoration- Initiated Prayer

Think of an aspect of God's character. [Feel free to use phrases of adoration from Scripture]

Lord, you are...

_____

_____

_____

_____

_____

How do you or in what ways have you fallen short of that perfect character you mentioned in the adoration section?

I confess that...

_____

_____

_____

_____

_____

In light of this fallibility in you, where are you asking the Lord to grow you? For which brother or sister in Christ might you also pray to grow in this area of fallibility?

Lord, I ask you to...

_____

_____

_____

_____

_____

In what ways can you give thanksgiving to God in relation to all of this?

Lord, I ask you to...

_____

_____

_____

_____

_____

Take a moment to pray what you have written, in the Name of Jesus. Allow Him to lead you back to Adoration, further Confession, more Supplication/Intercession, and Thanksgiving.

Non-Linear Prayer: Adoration-Initiated Prayer Graph

If you are more visual or non-linear, use the chart below to write out your prayer points.

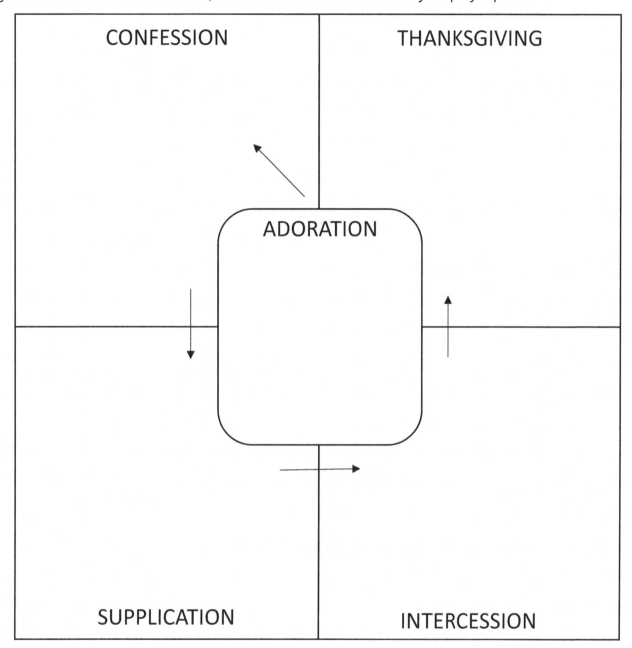

Week Forty-Three

Week Of:

PRAYER STUDY

Read the Prayer: *Psalm 74*

Does the person praying in this Scripture use words of adoration for the Lord? If so, what are they?

_____

_____

_____

_____

_____

Does the person praying in this Scripture confess their sin? If not, does there seem to be an immaturity in their prayer where they needed to grow or a situation in their life that would warrant confession?

_____

_____

_____

_____

_____

Does the person praying in Scripture offer thanksgiving to God? If there is ample information about their life in the Bible, are there things in their story for which they should've been thankful?

_____

_____

_____

_____

_____

What, if any, are the requests they are making to God for themselves?

_____

_____

_____

_____

_____

What, if any, are the requests they are making on behalf of others?

_____

_____

_____

_____

_____

Your Prayer: The Confession- Initiated Prayer

Currently, where do you sense you are falling short of the glory of God? (Romans 3:23)

Lord, I confess...

_____

_____

_____

_____

_____

What does God's perfect character look like in contrast to your falling short?

But Lord, Your Word says that You are...

_____

_____

_____

_____

_____

What thanksgiving might you offer to God in regard to His mercy toward you or His offer of redemption in Christ or His patience with you? How has He specifically exhibited those things?

I thank you that...

_____

_____

_____

_____

_____

In what ways can you ask Him to grow you in grace? In what ways can you pray for particular unbelievers to recognize their own sin and trust in Christ alone?

Lord, I ask you to...

_____

_____

_____

_____

_____

Take a moment to pray what you have written, in the Name of Jesus. Allow Him to lead you back to further Confession, Adoration, Thanksgiving, and more Supplication/Intercession.

Non-Linear Prayer: Confession-Initiated Prayer Graph

If you are more visual or non-linear, use the chart below to write out your prayer points.

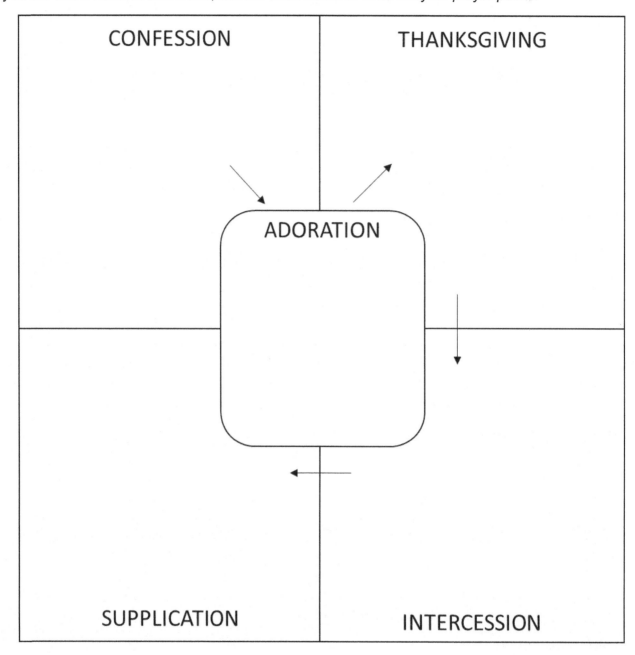

Week Forty-Four

Week Of:

PRAYER STUDY

Read the Prayer: *Psalm 74*

Does the person praying in this Scripture use words of adoration for the Lord? If so, what are they?

_____

_____

_____

_____

Does the person praying in this Scripture confess their sin? If not, does there seem to be an immaturity in their prayer where they needed to grow or a situation in their life that would warrant confession?

_____

_____

_____

_____

Does the person praying in Scripture offer thanksgiving to God? If there is ample information about their life in the Bible, are there things in their story for which they should've been thankful?

_____

_____

_____

_____

What, if any, are the requests they are making to God for themselves?

_____

_____

_____

_____

What, if any, are the requests they are making on behalf of others?

_____

_____

_____

_____

Your Prayer: The Supplication/Intersession- Initiated Prayer

What is the most pressing need you or someone else is struggling with?

Lord, I ask...

_____
_____
_____
_____
_____

How might you thank God for ways He has answered your prayers in the past?

Thank you for...

_____
_____
_____
_____
_____

What character of God do you need to be reminded of in light of your supplication/intercession request?

You have shown us in Your Word that You are...

_____
_____
_____
_____
_____

What might you need to confess in regard to all of this? Is there an attitude of doubt that the Lord will do and be all He has said He will do and be, etc?

Forgive me...

_____
_____
_____
_____
_____

Take a moment to pray what you have written, in the Name of Jesus. Allow Him to lead you back to Supplication/Intercession, Thanksgiving, Adoration, and further Confession.

Non-Linear Prayer: Supplication/Intercession-Initiated Prayer Graph

If you are more visual or non-linear, use the chart below to write out your prayer points.

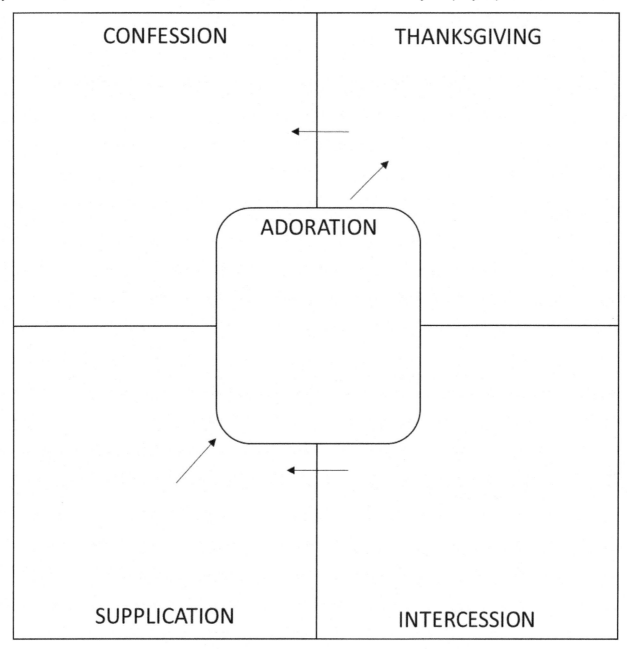

Week Forty-Five

Week Of:

PRAYER STUDY

Read the Prayer: *Psalm 50*

Does the person praying in this Scripture use words of adoration for the Lord? If so, what are they?

_____

_____

_____

_____

_____

Does the person praying in this Scripture confess their sin? If not, does there seem to be an immaturity in their prayer where they needed to grow or a situation in their life that would warrant confession?

_____

_____

_____

_____

_____

Does the person praying in Scripture offer thanksgiving to God? If there is ample information about their life in the Bible, are there things in their story for which they should've been thankful?

_____

_____

_____

_____

_____

What, if any, are the requests they are making to God for themselves?

_____

_____

_____

_____

_____

What, if any, are the requests they are making on behalf of others?

_____

_____

_____

_____

_____

Your Prayer: The Thanksgiving- Initiated Prayer

What is something for which you are thankful? (Write it in the form of a prayer)

Dear Lord, thank you...

_____
_____
_____
_____
_____

What aspect of God's character did He show through what He provided?

Lord, you are...

_____
_____
_____
_____
_____

In light of God's character and His provision, what about your actions or attitude of your own heart do you need to confess?

Lord, forgive me...

_____
_____
_____
_____
_____

What do you need to ask Him to do within you or for you or for others in light of all of the above?

Lord, I ask you to...

_____
_____
_____
_____
_____

Take a moment to pray what you have written, in the Name of Jesus. Allow Him to lead you back to Thanksgiving, Adoration, further Confession, or more Supplication/Intercession.

Non-Linear Prayer: Thanksgiving-Initiated Prayer Graph

If you are more visual or non-linear, use the chart below to write out your prayer points.

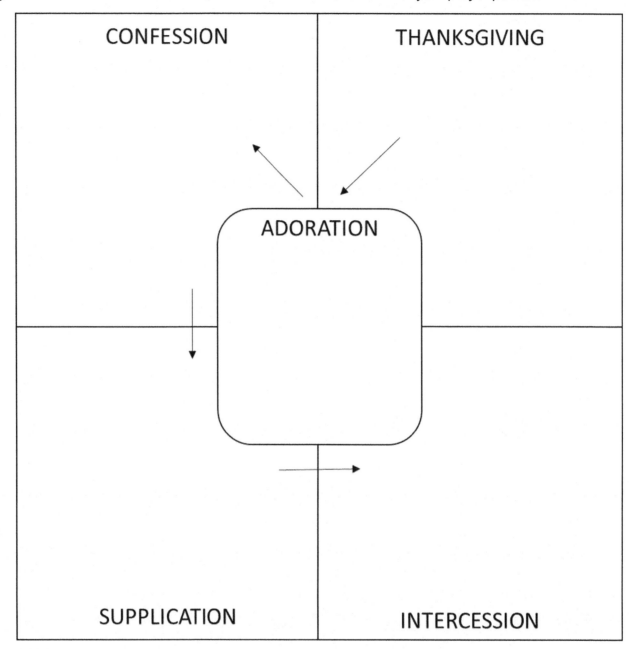

Week Forty-Six

Week Of:

PRAYER STUDY

Read the Prayer: *Psalm 61*

Does the person praying in this Scripture use words of adoration for the Lord? If so, what are they?

_____

_____

_____

_____

_____

Does the person praying in this Scripture confess their sin? If not, does there seem to be an immaturity in their prayer where they needed to grow or a situation in their life that would warrant confession?

_____

_____

_____

_____

_____

Does the person praying in Scripture offer thanksgiving to God? If there is ample information about their life in the Bible, are there things in their story for which they should've been thankful?

_____

_____

_____

_____

_____

What, if any, are the requests they are making to God for themselves?

_____

_____

_____

_____

_____

What, if any, are the requests they are making on behalf of others?

_____

_____

_____

_____

_____

Your Prayer: The Adoration- Initiated Prayer

Think of an aspect of God's character. [Feel free to use phrases of adoration from Scripture]

Lord, you are...

_____
_____
_____
_____
_____

How do you or in what ways have you fallen short of that perfect character you mentioned in the adoration section?

I confess that...

_____
_____
_____
_____
_____

In light of this fallibility in you, where are you asking the Lord to grow you? For which brother or sister in Christ might you also pray to grow in this area of fallibility?

Lord, I ask you to...

_____
_____
_____
_____
_____

In what ways can you give thanksgiving to God in relation to all of this?

Lord, I ask you to...

_____
_____
_____
_____
_____

Take a moment to pray what you have written, in the Name of Jesus. Allow Him to lead you back to Adoration, further Confession, more Supplication/Intercession, and Thanksgiving.

Non-Linear Prayer: Adoration-Initiated Prayer Graph

If you are more visual or non-linear, use the chart below to write out your prayer points.

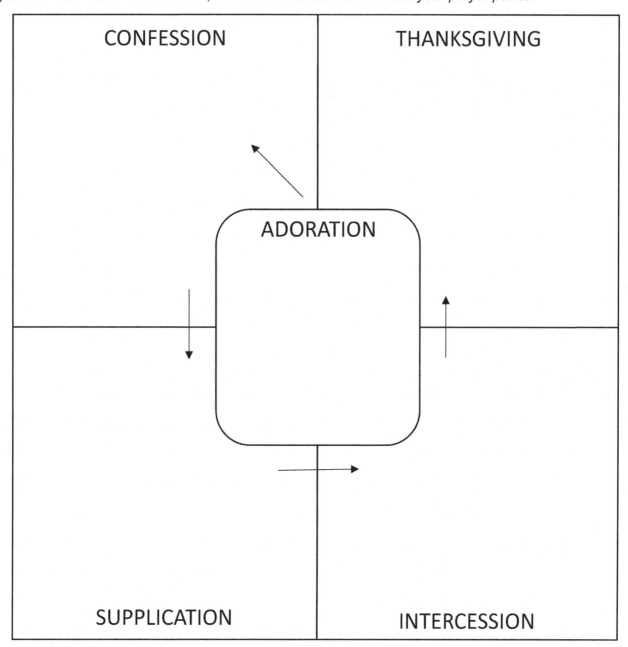

Week Forty-Seven

PRAYER STUDY

Read the Prayer: *Psalm 132*

Does the person praying in this Scripture use words of adoration for the Lord? If so, what are they?

_____

_____

_____

_____

_____

Does the person praying in this Scripture confess their sin? If not, does there seem to be an immaturity in their prayer where they needed to grow or a situation in their life that would warrant confession?

_____

_____

_____

_____

_____

Does the person praying in Scripture offer thanksgiving to God? If there is ample information about their life in the Bible, are there things in their story for which they should've been thankful?

_____

_____

_____

_____

_____

What, if any, are the requests they are making to God for themselves?

_____

_____

_____

_____

What, if any, are the requests they are making on behalf of others?

_____

_____

_____

_____

Your Prayer: The Confession- Initiated Prayer

Currently, where do you sense you are falling short of the glory of God? (Romans 3:23)

Lord, I confess…

_____

_____

_____

_____

_____

What does God's perfect character look like in contrast to your falling short?

But Lord, Your Word says that You are…

_____

_____

_____

_____

_____

What thanksgiving might you offer to God in regard to His mercy toward you or His offer of redemption in Christ or His patience with you? How has He specifically exhibited those things?

I thank you that…

_____

_____

_____

_____

_____

In what ways can you ask Him to grow you in grace? In what ways can you pray for particular unbelievers to recognize their own sin and trust in Christ alone?

Lord, I ask you to…

_____

_____

_____

_____

_____

Take a moment to pray what you have written, in the Name of Jesus. Allow Him to lead you back to further Confession, Adoration, Thanksgiving, and more Supplication/Intercession.

Non-Linear Prayer: Confession-Initiated Prayer Graph

If you are more visual or non-linear, use the chart below to write out your prayer points.

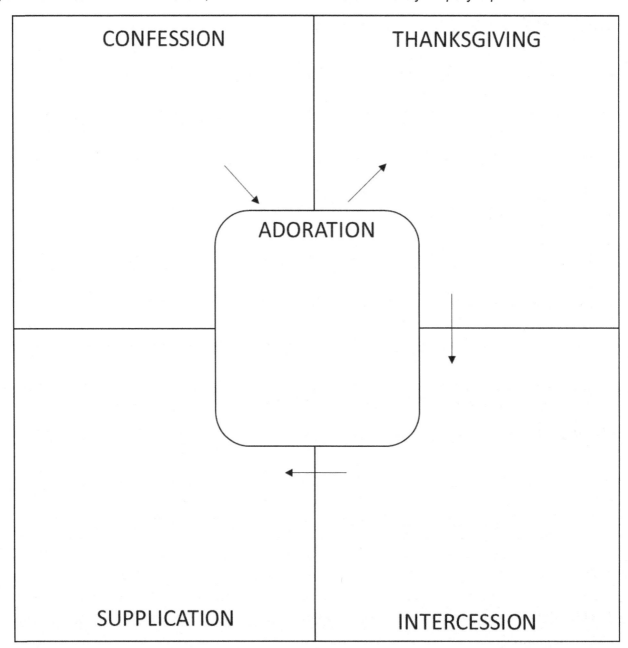

Week Forty-Eight

Week Of:

PRAYER STUDY

Read the Prayer: *Psalm 86*

Does the person praying in this Scripture use words of adoration for the Lord? If so, what are they?

_____

_____

_____

_____

_____

Does the person praying in this Scripture confess their sin? If not, does there seem to be an immaturity in their prayer where they needed to grow or a situation in their life that would warrant confession?

_____

_____

_____

_____

_____

Does the person praying in Scripture offer thanksgiving to God? If there is ample information about their life in the Bible, are there things in their story for which they should've been thankful?

_____

_____

_____

_____

_____

What, if any, are the requests they are making to God for themselves?

_____

_____

_____

_____

_____

What, if any, are the requests they are making on behalf of others?

_____

_____

_____

_____

_____

Your Prayer: The Supplication/Intersession- Initiated Prayer

What is the most pressing need you or someone else is struggling with?

Lord, I ask...

_____

_____

_____

_____

_____

How might you thank God for ways He has answered your prayers in the past?

Thank you for...

_____

_____

_____

_____

_____

What character of God do you need to be reminded of in light of your supplication/intercession request?

You have shown us in Your Word that You are...

_____

_____

_____

_____

_____

What might you need to confess in regard to all of this? Is there an attitude of doubt that the Lord will do and be all He has said He will do and be, etc?

Forgive me...

_____

_____

_____

_____

_____

Take a moment to pray what you have written, in the Name of Jesus. Allow Him to lead you back to Supplication/Intercession, Thanksgiving, Adoration, and further Confession.

Non-Linear Prayer: Supplication/Intercession-Initiated Prayer Graph

If you are more visual or non-linear, use the chart below to write out your prayer points.

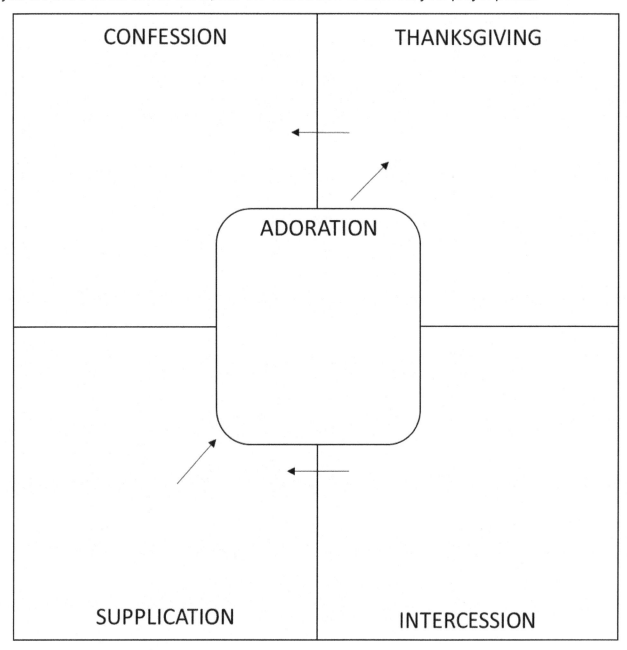

Week Forty-Nine

Week Of:

PRAYER STUDY

Read the Prayer: *Psalm 65*

Does the person praying in this Scripture use words of adoration for the Lord? If so, what are they?

_____

_____

_____

_____

_____

Does the person praying in this Scripture confess their sin? If not, does there seem to be an immaturity in their prayer where they needed to grow or a situation in their life that would warrant confession?

_____

_____

_____

_____

_____

Does the person praying in Scripture offer thanksgiving to God? If there is ample information about their life in the Bible, are there things in their story for which they should've been thankful?

_____

_____

_____

_____

_____

What, if any, are the requests they are making to God for themselves?

_____

_____

_____

_____

_____

What, if any, are the requests they are making on behalf of others?

_____

_____

_____

_____

_____

Your Prayer: The Thanksgiving- Initiated Prayer

What is something for which you are thankful? (Write it in the form of a prayer)

Dear Lord, thank you…

_____
_____
_____
_____
_____

What aspect of God's character did He show through what He provided?

Lord, you are…

_____
_____
_____
_____
_____

In light of God's character and His provision, what about your actions or attitude of your own heart do you need to confess?

Lord, forgive me…

_____
_____
_____
_____
_____

What do you need to ask Him to do within you or for you or for others in light of all of the above?

Lord, I ask you to…

_____
_____
_____
_____
_____

Take a moment to pray what you have written, in the Name of Jesus. Allow Him to lead you back to Thanksgiving, Adoration, further Confession, or more Supplication/Intercession.

Non-Linear Prayer: Thanksgiving-Initiated Prayer Graph

If you are more visual or non-linear, use the chart below to write out your prayer points.

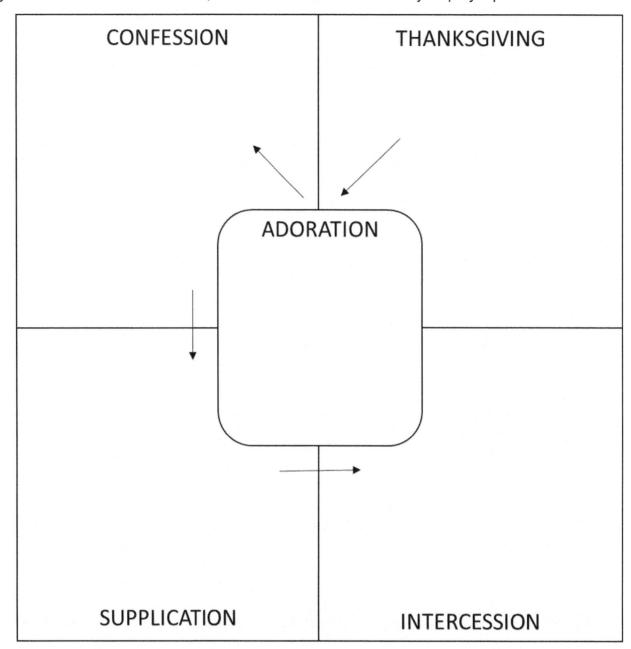

Week Fifty

Week Of:

PRAYER STUDY

Read the Prayer: *Psalm 44*

Does the person praying in this Scripture use words of adoration for the Lord? If so, what are they?

_____

_____

_____

_____

Does the person praying in this Scripture confess their sin? If not, does there seem to be an immaturity in their prayer where they needed to grow or a situation in their life that would warrant confession?

_____

_____

_____

_____

Does the person praying in Scripture offer thanksgiving to God? If there is ample information about their life in the Bible, are there things in their story for which they should've been thankful?

_____

_____

_____

_____

What, if any, are the requests they are making to God for themselves?

_____

_____

_____

_____

What, if any, are the requests they are making on behalf of others?

_____

_____

_____

_____

Your Prayer: The Adoration- Initiated Prayer

Think of an aspect of God's character. [Feel free to use phrases of adoration from Scripture]

Lord, you are...

_____
_____
_____
_____
_____

How do you or in what ways have you fallen short of that perfect character you mentioned in the adoration section?

I confess that...

_____
_____
_____
_____
_____

In light of this fallibility in you, where are you asking the Lord to grow you? For which brother or sister in Christ might you also pray to grow in this area of fallibility?

Lord, I ask you to...

_____
_____
_____
_____
_____

In what ways can you give thanksgiving to God in relation to all of this?

Lord, I ask you to...

_____
_____
_____
_____
_____

Take a moment to pray what you have written, in the Name of Jesus. Allow Him to lead you back to Adoration, further Confession, more Supplication/Intercession, and Thanksgiving.

Non-Linear Prayer: Adoration-Initiated Prayer Graph

If you are more visual or non-linear, use the chart below to write out your prayer points.

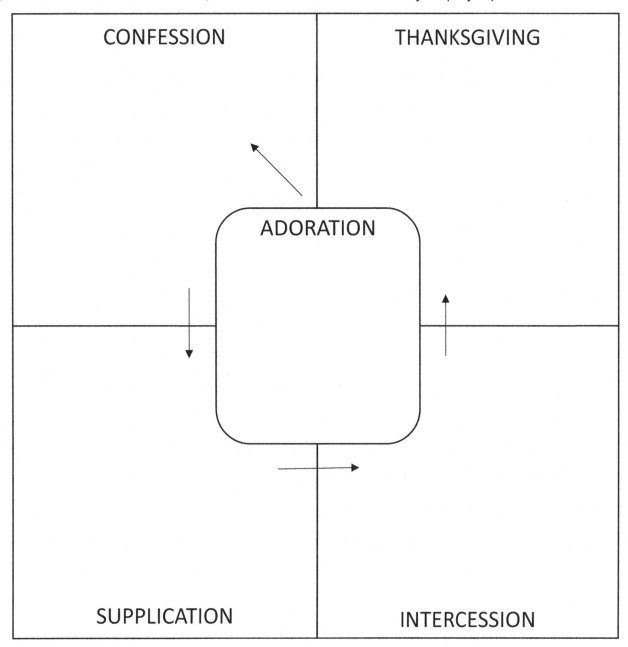

Week Fifty-One

PRAYER STUDY

Read the Prayer: *Psalm 55*

Does the person praying in this Scripture use words of adoration for the Lord? If so, what are they?

_____

_____

_____

_____

_____

Does the person praying in this Scripture confess their sin? If not, does there seem to be an immaturity in their prayer where they needed to grow or a situation in their life that would warrant confession?

_____

_____

_____

_____

_____

Does the person praying in Scripture offer thanksgiving to God? If there is ample information about their life in the Bible, are there things in their story for which they should've been thankful?

_____

_____

_____

_____

_____

What, if any, are the requests they are making to God for themselves?

_____

_____

_____

_____

_____

What, if any, are the requests they are making on behalf of others?

_____

_____

_____

_____

_____

Your Prayer: The Confession- Initiated Prayer

Currently, where do you sense you are falling short of the glory of God? (Romans 3:23)

Lord, I confess...

_____
_____
_____
_____
_____

What does God's perfect character look like in contrast to your falling short?

But Lord, Your Word says that You are...

_____
_____
_____
_____
_____

What thanksgiving might you offer to God in regard to His mercy toward you or His offer of redemption in Christ or His patience with you? How has He specifically exhibited those things?

I thank you that...

_____
_____
_____
_____
_____

In what ways can you ask Him to grow you in grace? In what ways can you pray for particular unbelievers to recognize their own sin and trust in Christ alone?

Lord, I ask you to...

_____
_____
_____
_____
_____

Take a moment to pray what you have written, in the Name of Jesus. Allow Him to lead you back to further Confession, Adoration, Thanksgiving, and more Supplication/Intercession.

Non-Linear Prayer: Confession-Initiated Prayer Graph

If you are more visual or non-linear, use the chart below to write out your prayer points.

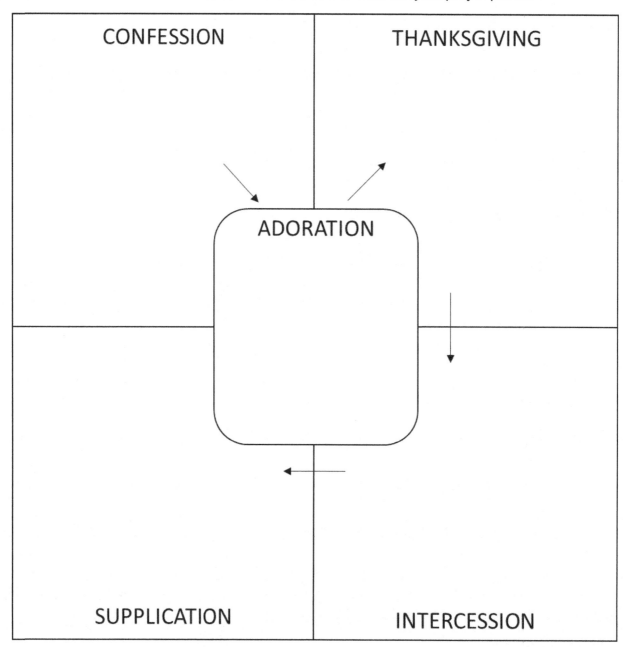

Week Fifty-Two

Week Of:

PRAYER STUDY

Read the Prayer: *Psalm 85*

Does the person praying in this Scripture use words of adoration for the Lord? If so, what are they?

_____

_____

_____

_____

_____

Does the person praying in this Scripture confess their sin? If not, does there seem to be an immaturity in their prayer where they needed to grow or a situation in their life that would warrant confession?

_____

_____

_____

_____

_____

Does the person praying in Scripture offer thanksgiving to God? If there is ample information about their life in the Bible, are there things in their story for which they should've been thankful?

_____

_____

_____

_____

_____

What, if any, are the requests they are making to God for themselves?

_____

_____

_____

_____

_____

What, if any, are the requests they are making on behalf of others?

_____

_____

_____

_____

_____

Your Prayer: The Supplication/Intersession- Initiated Prayer

What is the most pressing need you or someone else is struggling with?

Lord, I ask...

_____
_____
_____
_____
_____

How might you thank God for ways He has answered your prayers in the past?

Thank you for...

_____
_____
_____
_____
_____

What character of God do you need to be reminded of in light of your supplication/intercession request?

You have shown us in Your Word that You are...

_____
_____
_____
_____
_____

What might you need to confess in regard to all of this? Is there an attitude of doubt that the Lord will do and be all He has said He will do and be, etc?

Forgive me...

_____
_____
_____
_____
_____

Take a moment to pray what you have written, in the Name of Jesus. Allow Him to lead you back to Supplication/Intercession, Thanksgiving, Adoration, and further Confession.

Non-Linear Prayer: Supplication/Intercession-Initiated Prayer Graph

If you are more visual or non-linear, use the chart below to write out your prayer points.

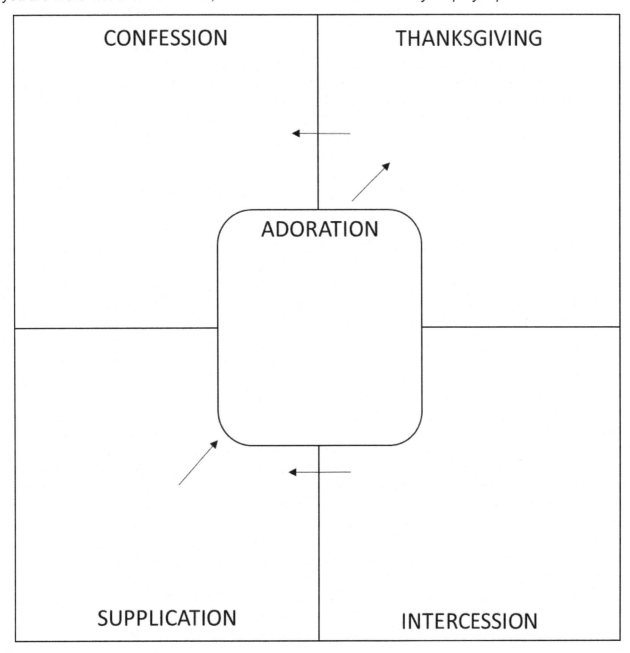

For more resources like this, follow my page on Facebook at: Facebook.com/zacharyfcarden

Made in the USA
Columbia, SC
11 January 2020